A Guide
to a Man's
Spiritual Health

C. DENNIS WILLIAMS

WESTBOW®
PRESS
A DIVISION OF THOMAS NELSON
& ZONDERVAN

Scripture taken from the Holy Bible, NEW INTERNATIONAL VERSION®. Copyright © 1973, 1978, 1984 by Biblica, Inc. All rights reserved worldwide. Used by permission. NEW INTERNATIONAL VERSION® and NIV® are registered trademarks of Biblica, Inc. Use of either trademark for the offering of goods or services requires the prior written consent of Biblica US, Inc.

WestBow Press books may be ordered through booksellers or by contacting:

WestBow Press
A Division of Thomas Nelson & Zondervan
1663 Liberty Drive
Bloomington, IN 47403
www.westbowpress.com
1 (866) 928-1240

Because of the dynamic nature of the Internet, any web addresses or links contained in this book may have changed since publication and may no longer be valid. The views expressed in this work are solely those of the author and do not necessarily reflect the views of the publisher, and the publisher hereby disclaims any responsibility for them.

Any people depicted in stock imagery provided by Thinkstock are models, and such images are being used for illustrative purposes only. Certain stock imagery © Thinkstock.

ISBN: 978-1-4908-7155-4 (sc)
ISBN: 978-1-4908-7157-8 (hc)
ISBN: 978-1-4908-7156-1 (e)

Library of Congress Control Number: 2015903315

Print information available on the last page.

WestBow Press rev. date: 03/18/2015

Contents

To my faithful and loving wife, Yvette, who encourages me every day and has encouraged me for years to publish my sermons and other writings. My love for her grows greater every day.

Introduction

Physical and Spiritual Health Connection

I want to begin by countering any idea that this is another book about health and medicine written by a physician. I am not a physician but a member of the clergy and a professor who is concerned about the spiritual component of all humanity, the soul.

So much emphasis in today's society is on a man's physical strength. The ability to lift heavy loads, be tough, be macho, and endure seems to be what's expected of men. So many commercials tout performance-enhancing drugs, all of which are directed toward the psyche and physicality of men. As men, we need to be more concerned about our health, not just our physical strength.

Now that I am in my early fifties, I have become increasingly conscientious about my health. The phobia of seeing a doctor is suddenly no longer a factor for me, and eating healthful foods and exercising are no longer struggles and burdens. In fact, I look forward to exercising and enjoying lighter meals such as salads, soups, and oatmeal, especially since doing so can add to my longevity and help prevent serious illnesses such as cardiac arrest.

As I read about men's health and speak to physicians, the consensus is the same; some diseases affect men more than they do women, including heart disease, cancer, injuries, strokes, and HIV/AIDS. The June 13, 2013, edition of *Providence Physicians* confirms this. Heart disease, the human immunodeficiency virus (HIV), and acquired immunodeficiency syndrome (AIDS) are at the top of the list, and HIV/AIDS is known as the silent killer.

HIV can affect men without them knowing it. HIV causes AIDS and is acquired through unprotected sex or the use of infected needles. Some diseases are more prominent in men based on their ethnicity; nearly one in five black men has been or will be diagnosed with prostate cancer, the fourth most common reason for death for black men in the United States. Early detection through prostate cancer screenings and yearly visits to physicians is the best preventative measure.

I am convinced that God has called us as men to be priests, protectors, and providers for our family and friends. As priests, we are called to lead our families in prayer, take our families to church, and allow our families to watch us participate in active ministry, teaching, volunteering, and mentoring other young men in our churches and communities.

As protectors, we have been assigned by God to serve as watchmen on the wall to alert the city of danger as did the prophets of old and to pray unusual and demonic spirits away from those we love and from where we live.

As providers, our duty is to provide for our children and families spiritual and physical inheritances and provide others with our examples of men with disciplined prayer lives and balanced moral lives.

All of this causes me to ask, is there a synergy between a man's physical and spiritual relationship? I say yes. It's no coincidence that hospitals, nursing homes, treatment centers, and other places of therapy and recovery have chaplains, many of whom are full-time because there is a connection between prayer and medicine, religion and faith.

Having been a pastor for twenty-nine years, I have listened to countless testimonials from parishioners who have been diagnosed by doctors with incurable illnesses but who prayed to God and over time were miraculously healed. Many doctors are keenly aware of a power that is higher and stronger than medicine, and because of that knowledge, it's common for doctors to ask patients about their faith lives and the support systems they might provide in times of crisis.

More and more physicians and nurses concur that prayer, meditation, regular church attendance, and consistent readings of the Bible are benefits to health that medicine, science, and any other medicinal influences cannot explain. With this in mind, I have written sermons and writings directed at men; these writings will equip men with the spiritual tools that will compel them to hunger and thirst for righteousness and encourage them to consider their faith, spirituality, and overall prayer life. The health of a man begins with his spiritual health.

I pray all my readers will find themselves in these biblical narratives and learn from their mistakes. More important, I want them to experience their faith, for healthy men are cleansed from the inside out.

One of the highlights of this book is a sermon I wrote and preached shortly after Barack Obama was elected president. This message was shared as an inaugural sermon in honor of President Obama and is filed in the Library of Congress with the title "Providential Prayers for Presidential Leadership." May this book illuminate men's inner beings, inspire their faith, and ignite revolutions in their hearts that will alter the way they love their families and treat humankind. Let's follow in the path of Jesus lest we die from malnourishment. Enjoy these messages in *A Guide to a Man's Spiritual Health*.

Chapter 1

Gaius: The Epitome of a Spiritually Healthy Life

3 John 1–8

Kent Crockett, a noted Christian author and theologian, wrote, "God is not interested in us being famous but faithful." Kent Crockett wrote, "Famous is how we appear in the world's eye, but faithful is how we appear in God's eyes."

His lines took on new meaning for me as I learned some time ago of a new reality show, *Crown Chasers*. In it, women between the ages of thirty and fifty-two participate in hubris, cutthroat methods, and chicanery to win a crown in the world of beauty pageantry. It follows the lives of a handful of these women and shows us how they juggle families, marriages, and careers to win the crown. They are willing to do whatever they need to do to become famous.

What we need in the church are more crown chasers, people who, unlike the women in the show, will not stoop to politics or blackmail to achieve crowns but will attempt to get them through service, faithfulness, honor, and devotion. John the Revelator said it better than I ever could have in Revelation 2:10: "Be thou faithful even unto the point of death, and I will give you the crown of Life." Faithful believers are servants, not stars. Stars like the limelight, but servants are guided by the light of Christ!

In the text before us, we find John the disciple, whom Jesus loved, writing as the elder of a church of which Gaius—a layman, not a preacher—was a member. Gaius was a common name, especially during the first century Roman Empire. In fact, there are three other Gaiuses in the Bible: Gaius of Derbe, Gaius of Corinth, and Gaius of Macedonia. Gaius, John's friend, was someone whose life is worth imitating. He was a man of deep conviction; he was very principled, and he was saved. John held him in such high commendation that he addressed this letter to him, a first for John.

Gaius was a leader in his lay organization, was kind to everybody, loved God deeply, and treated the members of his local church with honor. He showed leadership in his church. John so revered him that he called him "dear friend" at least four times.

We need more church members like Gaius, people who get along with everybody, even those who succeed in making themselves almost impossible to get along with. We need more church members who, like Gaius, won't socialize with just a select group because of their prominence but will do so with everybody. Gaius was an icon of Christianity.

It is clear from verse 2 that though his spiritual life was secure, he had been dealing with some kind of physical illness. John said to him in verse 2, "I pray that you may enjoy good health even as your soul is getting along well." The KJV reads, "I pray that you may prosper in all things and be in health just as your soul prospers." John was saying that he wanted Gaius's physical health to be as blessed as his spiritual health.

When children of God are spiritually prosperous, the Devil will attack their physical bodies because their spiritual lives are off limits to him. He can attack the believer but not the believer's anointing, gift, or spirituality.

The Bible declares in Proverbs 10:22, "The blessing of the Lord brings wealth, and adds no trouble to it." God won't give us a gift to bring confusion. That's why anytime people are doing well spiritually and the Holy Spirit comes upon them, the first thing that will happen is sickness will try to come in and disrupt their blessing. If we don't believe it, look at the woman in Luke 13:11. She had what the Bible calls a spirit of infirmity. For eighteen years, she was bent over, and in verse 16 of that chapter, Jesus said that Satan had her bound.

But the woman was in the synagogue when Jesus was teaching. The Devil had attacked her physically because he couldn't attack her spiritually. That's why we have to stop missing church because of a cough or cold. If we do, we have lost and the Devil has won. We should get ourselves up, take some cough syrup or some castor oil, shake it off, and tell the Devil he won't get the victory because Isaiah says that by Jesus' stripes we are healed.

Gaius was blessed with spiritual prosperity; he was faithful and loved God so much that his personality attracted people rather than repelled them. Some people don't know how to talk to people, but Gaius wasn't one of them, as is evident in verse 3. John was complimentary of Gaius and said it gave him great joy to have some of the brothers tell him that he was faithful in the truth and that he walked in the truth. He lived in such a way that others were willing to testify on his behalf.

Can we find such witnesses for ourselves? Some were watching the righteous way Gaius lived, walked, and talked and how he treated others to the extent that they were willing to testify on his behalf to John. When we live right, God will always raise up somebody to speak on our behalf. We won't have to always speak for ourselves, we won't have to boast about our service, and we won't have to pat ourselves on the back, and just when we think we've been forgotten, somebody somewhere will show up and say, "You helped me when you didn't even know you were helping me!" God allowed others to show up in 1 Kings 19:5. When Elijah was running from Jezebel, he slept under a juniper tree. An angel showed up and said, "Eat. You need strength for the journey."

But there is another aspect of this Christian gentleman's life we can see in verses 5 to 8. Gaius was hospitable; he knew how to treat others. He opened his doors and entertained others. He understood that when the Lord blesses us with a home, it is not just for us; he expects us to do ministry in our homes. In the same way, we can't buy a new car and never offer anyone a ride home. Some preachers, missionaries, and evangelists were itinerant, and Gaius, even without knowing them, opened his home to them because of who they were.

We have to know some things about this era before we volunteer our homes too quickly. When people traveled back then, there were few hotels or shelters. The best place for a traveling preacher to rest was at someone's home. When people traveled, they carried all their necessities—pallets for their beds, clothes, cooking utensils, and so on.

We can thus understand why Jesus said foxes had holes and birds had nests but the Son of God had no place to lay his head. If we were going to house such people, we'd need to be able to handle all their stuff, and we should ask ourselves, "Can we handle all their stuff?" Gaius was willing to open his home not just for them but for all of their stuff too. Homes established for ministry don't worry about somebody else's stuff ruining their images.

One of the many things I love about God is that he loves us in spite of all our stuff—our attitudes, negative dispositions, and deceptive politics. He looks through all of that and always sees something worth saving.

Please be patient with me. God is not through with me yet. He is still molding me; he is still shaping and making me. Work on me, Lord. Work on my mind so I can think right. Work on my eyes so I can see right. Work on my ears so I can hear you speak!

Chapter 2

Not in My House

Mark 3:27

A little boy lived with his family in a trailer. One day, someone asked him, "Don't you wish you had a real home?" The boy responded, "We have a home. We just don't have a house to put it in." A house and a home are different, aren't they? A house is just a physical structure made of brick, stone, and wood. It can be large or small and doesn't actually need anyone inside to be a house, but a home is an atmosphere of shelter, acceptance, and unconditional love.

Any decent contractor can build a house, but only God can build a home. Many of our homes have become nothing but houses because of what we have allowed inside them. "Not in my house" is what you'll hear from those basketball players who have good interior defense and are able to block shots. In some cases, because of a lack of defense, we have allowed the "saggy pants" syndrome into our homes by letting our children run the place. Because of a lack of defense, we have allowed people to move in with us who we aren't married to, giving them the same rights as a spouse. Because of a lack of defense, we have allowed people to enter our homes and bring along lifestyles that are unbecoming for Christians. Because of a lack of defense! I proclaim that not only will defense win games, it will also save our homes.

That's why in Ephesians we're told to put on the whole armor of God. Everything in that armor except for the sword is for our defense.

Everybody say "Defense!" Who will say, "As for me and my house, we will serve the Lord"? God is looking for a few good men.

This concise text is simply about spiritual warfare. The scribes were on their way from Jerusalem and arrived shortly after Jesus had been doing some healing (Matthew 12:29). The scribes acknowledged that Jesus had power, but they insinuated he was working miracles in the name of Beelzebub, a name for the Devil that means "master of the house."

Jesus picked up on this meaning and told a parable about a strong man guarding his house. To rob the house, someone would first have to overcome the strong man. If it was by the power of Satan that Jesus had cast out the demons that meant Satan was fighting Satan, and a house divided against itself cannot stand. That would mean Satan's kingdom would have been on the verge of collapse.

Let's look for a moment at this small fragment of verse 27, which is a parable in itself. Satan in this text was the strong man, his house was the realm of sin, his possessions were people, and demons were his agents. Jesus' point was that no one could enter the strongman's realm to carry off anything unless he first bound the strongman. Satan was the strong man, but Jesus was the stronger man.

There will always be a strong man, and every man needs a stronger man, one who has already endured, one who has already experienced what he is going through right now, one who knows this is what Paul meant in Galatians 6:1, where he said in essence, "Brothers, if someone is caught in sin, you who are spiritual should restore him gently, but watch yourself lest you are tempted. Restore him, but don't cover up for him. Don't lie to his spouse for him. Don't give him money for his addiction. Restore him by getting in his face and saying, 'Brother, you can't come to church with alcohol on your breath. This is God's house, and God says not in my house!'" If we don't this, we are not restorers and repairers of the breach like Isaiah 58 but codependents living in denial.

According to this verse, we have to notice that the strong man has a house. If we have established that the strong man is Satan, is the strongman's house at our address? We need to communicate to Satan in a resounding way and tell him he has the wrong address! If you think you can come home at 2:00 or 3:00 a.m. with an attitude, if you think you're going to walk around the house, cussing and fussing, if you think you can lie in bed until noon and then walk around the house with your pajamas on instead of going to work, you're at the wrong address! Get your blessed assurance up and get a job!

We have to say as Jesus did in Matthew 21 that his Father's house was a house of prayer but others had turned it into a den of thieves. Have our homes become houses of prayer or comfortable environments for thieves? Our homes should be the pit stop on our Christian races. It's the place we should be able to go in addition to church on Sunday morning to get filled up; it should be a place of fellowship, prayer, and Christian service.

This strong man is trying to take over our homes. How does this strong man get in our homes? Because we have allowed him to trespass? It's time to say "No trespassing!" Ephesians 4:27 tells us, "Do not give the Devil a foothold." If we ever do, we have given him a way into our homes. If there is anger in our homes, we have given him a foothold. If there is abuse in our homes, we have given him a foothold. When we let bootleg DVDs into our houses, we have given him a foothold. If we have been buying things off the street with no receipts, we have given him a foothold. And now that he is in our houses, it's going to be hard to get him out. That's why there is so much hell in many of our homes and even in churches. A church can have a lot of hell in it not because its members are bad but because a bad spirit has been festering all these years and the Devil has gained a foothold. Well, what we have to do is get some oil and kick him out in the name of Jesus, and if he's in our homes, we have to do the same thing all in the name of Jesus.

According to John 10:10, the Devil comes to steal, kill, and destroy; he comes to take our possessions. He breaks into people's houses to steal their goods, not his. He comes into our homes to take our possessions, which include anything he can get, control, and manipulate, including our minds, our sense of self-worth, dignity, self-respect, our finances, our families. I want every believer today to say to the enemy, "I want my stuff back. Give me my stuff back!" We need to tell him we want it all back, and if he doesn't, we have to just take it back ourselves. That's why Matthew 11:12 says, "From the days of John the Baptist until now; the kingdom of heaven has been forcefully advancing, and forceful men lay hold of it."

Sometimes, we have to fight for it. Jesus said we had to tie him up, which means we must bind him, and after that, we should tell the Lord we want to be wrapped up, tied up and tangled all up in him. The Lord wants to tie us up so tight that doubt can't get in, tie us up so tight that denial can't get in, so tight that lying can't get in.

Chapter 3

Lose the Ego

Judges 15:16

Another word for *ego* in the biblical sense is pride. We can psychoanalyze it as much as we want and give it all kinds of mental scrutiny. We can try to make it some deep psychological phenomenon, but the Bible simply calls it pride, and pride has been the culprit in so many of the atrocities and problems we are dealing with. Annika Sorenson, the first woman in fifty years to play in a PGA golf tournament (it had been restricted to men), found herself contending with the issue of pride; men were too proud to allow a woman to play with them because their egos would not let them play golf with women for fear of what they would look like if they lost.

We can see the ego syndrome in athletes who pout like children if they aren't paid millions, and make no mistake about it—wherever there is an ego, a fall will shortly follow, because Proverbs 16:18 tells us pride goes before the destruction. People with big egos run their mouths a lot, but all they're really doing is setting themselves up to be challenged and ultimately defeated.

Before the 2001–2002 NFL football season, Warren Sapp, the all-pro defensive lineman for the Tampa Bay Buccaneers, boasted that he would set the record for the most sacks that year, and with over sixteen sacks, it looked like he might do it. But before the season was over, a new record had been set by Michael Strahan—twenty-two sacks.

In 1927, Babe Ruth hit his sixtieth home run, and after the game, he pranced around the dugout, boasting, "Let's see somebody beat that." Well, it took a while, but Roger Maris did, and then Mark McGuire, Sammy Sosa, and Bobby Bonds all did. A person with pride is a person with a big ego who will cause us, according to Romans 12:3, to start thinking more highly of ourselves than we ought to.

Many men have big egos, and if they don't lose them, they will be difficult to live with. As I see it, the problem is not with losing the ego but what we replace it with. I want to help all brothers who are suffering from big ego syndrome. Yes, it exists; that's why when we are driving and we get lost, we are the last ones to pull in somewhere to ask for directions. That's why we don't like to lose to women in anything. As men, we sometimes live above our means because of the ego syndrome, and I want to show you how to overcome this problem by examining the persona of Samson. He had been raised up by God to rescue Israel from the Philistines. He was born to an elderly couple who thought they couldn't have children, but the wife received a visit from an angel, who informed her she would have a son named Samson who would be raised as a Nazirite. Nazirite is not to be confused with Nazarene, which means someone from Nazareth. Nazirites were people set apart, consecrated. They could not drink strong drink, touch dead bodies, or cut their hair. Samson was a Nazirite who had been blessed by God with superhuman strength, all of it in his hair, and even though he was able to save Israel from the Philistines, he had a tremendous ego. He was so strong but yet so weak.

One day, three thousand Philistines came to capture him, but Samson was bad, the baddest man in the Bible. Samson let them tie him up, making them think they had captured him, but he was playing possum. When the Spirit of the Lord came upon him, he broke those ropes, picked up the jawbone of a donkey, and killed one thousand men. But that was where his ego came in.

After he killed all those men, he made up a poem: "I have made donkeys of them. I have killed a thousand men." Now, it was God who had given him his strength; it was the Spirit of the Lord that had come upon him with power, but he never gave God credit for what he'd done; he didn't even mention God.

We men have become so independent that we have forgotten how to depend on God. Our egos have compelled us to ease God out. We ease him out of our family, our jobs, our finances, and our relationships, and we thus rob God of something that rightfully belongs to him, his glory. Isaiah 42:8 says, "I am the Lord, that is my name! I will not give my glory to another or my praise to idols." God is a loving God, and a healing God, but he is also a jealous God. He says in the Ten Commandments that there is one thing he will not share, and that is glory. So we need to be careful when we try to be just like him, because there are some things that belong only to the Lord. We must share, but the Lord does not have to share. Samson stole glory away from God, and God told me to tell the men and the women today he wants his glory back. So give it back!

He killed one thousand men with a donkey's jawbone but never thanked the Lord for sparing his life. We should never allow our egos to prevent us from saying thank you to God. James says that life is but a vapor that appears for a little while then vanishes.

Men, if you have served in Vietnam, the Persian Gulf, Iraq, or any other war and you made it home in one piece mentally and physically, you need to tell the Lord thank you. If you were in a car accident but ended up uninjured, you need to tell the Lord thank you. Psalm 30:5 tells us, "For his anger lasts only a moment, but his favor lasts a lifetime; weeping may remain for a night, but rejoicing comes in the morning." We always quote the latter part of that Scripture, "weeping may endure for a night, but joy comes in the morning," but the verse before that is just as powerful. His anger is but for a moment, but his favor lasts a lifetime. If God's anger lasted a lifetime, a whole lot of us would not be here. Think about what it would be like if God stayed mad at us every time we forgot to tell him thank you. Aren't you glad the Lord doesn't hold grudges?

I see something else in verse 16 and in the story of Samson's life. He was raised by God-fearing parents, but we don't see any indication that he had a meaningful spiritual life. We never heard of him giving

God praise, we never read about him worshipping God, and we never heard of him going to the temple on a regular basis. When a person has an ego, he is full of pride, and pride and religion go together, but pride and worship don't. Many people have religion but no worship; our churches are filled with people who just have religion. They flood our churches because they think that's the best place to get their egos fed. They can show off their outfits, display their musical talents, and lead this or that committee and receive compliments for all that, but church should not be a place for people to get their egos fed. It's a place reserved for worship.

If we want to know if we have an ego problem, we should ask ourselves how important worship is to us. Are we anxious to get to church on Sunday, or will any excuse do for not going? Do we feel empty when we miss church, or does it not bother us at all? God is looking for some good men free of ego, malice, envy, and drama and filled with love, power, and the Holy Spirit.

Chapter 4

The Tragedy of Sibling Entitlement

Luke 15:25–32

In August 2011, two siblings, Steven and Kathryn Miner, ages twenty-three and twenty, filed a $50,000 lawsuit against their mother. They claimed she'd been negligent, causing them emotional stress. They sued her for bad mothering—she hadn't sent her son care packages at college, she had refused to buy her daughter a homecoming dress, and she hadn't included any money in a birthday card to the son. Mind you, the children were being raised by their father in a $1.5 million home. The son presented in court as evidence the birthday card with a personal note from Mom that read, "Have a nice day, Love, Mom." The son was upset because the card contained no money, and the children stated in court that their mom had to be held accountable for her actions.

The judge threw the lawsuit out, saying that the attitude of the children was simply entitlement. Entitlement is when people feel that the world owes them something without having to do anything to earn it. After World War II, the United States experienced unprecedented economic growth, and the baby boomers (those born between 1946 and 1964) experienced the highest standard of living of any generation in history. The consumer market focused on this huge demographic and catered to their every need. Baby boomers passed this attitude down to their children—the promise of the American dream, a good job, good retirement—not taking into account that in order for the baby boomers to have such good lives, their parents had worked hard for decades.

Because of this entitlement syndrome, we are raising a generation of people who feel they are entitled to get whatever they want without working for it. They want the crown without the cross, but no cross, no crown. In 2 Thessalonians 3:10, we read, "For even when we were with you, we gave you this rule: 'If a man will not work, he shall not eat. You must get it the old-fashioned way.'"

Our emphasis today is on this elder brother. The younger brother, the Prodigal Son, represented the publicans and the sinners, for they represented in the Bible the sins of the flesh. The elder brother represented the scribes and the Pharisees, who represented sins of the spirit, or inward sins such as unloving spirits, an unwillingness to forgive, pride, and lust, and certainly that is what he exemplified as the elder brother. Because the younger brother had received his inheritance, the rest of the estate belonged to the elder son, but it was run by the father, who benefited from the profits. If the younger brother came back home, it would have confused the inheritance process, so the elder son was angry with his brother for coming home and angry with his father for welcoming him home. He got angry just as the Pharisees had gotten angry at Jesus for the message he was preaching.

The elder brother was angry because what he thought he was entitled to was in jeopardy. He thought he was entitled to his inheritance so much that he was not concerned about the loss of his brother. Sometimes in the church, we are guilty of living this entitlement syndrome, and we say that because we're a member of the pastor's family, we deserve this or that the rules don't apply to us, or we say that because our relatives' names are on the cornerstone, we can do whatever we want. We may think that because we've been members for forty years, we get to make all decisions and are entitled to be officers. We are so concerned about ourselves that we don't care about the lost, those who need saving, and how many have joined the church.

Feeling entitled can be a tragedy. We are all spiritual siblings, and we cannot be envious of somebody else's blessing, because like the Prodigal Son, the eldest son could have gotten the same blessings as his younger brother had, but the younger had done something the elder had not—the younger had asked for his inheritance. Yes, he was not entitled to it, but he got it prematurely. He wasted it, but he had asked for it.

In verses 25–27, when the older son was told the younger had come home, he got mad and refused to go to the celebration. He thought he was so entitled to something that he became a passive-aggressive party pooper. He pouted and grumbled outside, and the father had to stop enjoying the party to go outside and pacify him.

Don't you dare try to bring that mess into the church just because you can't run a program or didn't get voted in. Just because you weren't the chairperson doesn't mean you can sabotage the program. Instead of trying to bring everybody out, try going in and helping out. Try going in and serving the guests, try going in and celebrating by being a part of the festivities, for you will not always be the center of attention.

As the older son got close to home, he heard the music. That's the way our church services should be—so loud that the neighbors complain. But that's all right, because Isaiah 58:1 says, "Shout aloud and don't hold back, don't hold back your shout, don't hold back your dance, don't hold back your gift."

This elder son thought he was entitled to a party. We should never get upset at someone else's party; we should be so comfortable with what the Lord has done for us that we should throw ourselves a party, hire a DJ to play our favorite songs, send invitations to ourselves, RSVP ourselves, and celebrate our own accomplishments. If nobody wants to throw us a party, celebrate yourself.

David of the Old Testament taught us this lesson when in 1 Samuel 30:6, we read that he was greatly distressed because the men were talking about stoning him. Each one was bitter in spirit because his sons and daughters were blaming David, but verse 6 says David encouraged himself in the Lord. He started talking to himself, preaching to himself, singing to himself, humming to himself, and answering himself. Have you ever talked yourself out of a mess? You will make some; I know I will. You're not crazy, and I know I'm not, so talk to yourself and answer yourself.

The elder son concluded his little entitlement rant by saying in verses 28–32, "All these years I have been slaving for you and never asked you for anything." He saw his father as a master rather than a father, so he felt in bondage in his own house. But listen to the father's rebuttal: "Son, everything I have is yours" (verse 31). He was saying, "Stop there. I have enough to go around, so don't get a covetous spirit because someone has more than we have. Just know there's enough to go around."

Preachers don't have to fight over their pulpits; there are enough churches to go around, there are enough members for all of us. Members don't have to worry about titles and positions in the church because God has enough work to go around. Deuteronomy 6:10–11 says,

> When the Lord your God brings you into the land he swore to your fathers, to Abraham, Isaac, and Jacob, to give you a land with large, flourishing cities you did not build, houses filled with all kinds of good things you did not provide, wells you did not dig, and vineyards and olive groves you did not plant-then when you eat and are satisfied.

Well, there are some things we may not be entitled to, but there are some things that belong to us simply by association. Here it comes. Seek ye first the kingdom of God, and all these things shall be added unto you.

Chapter 5

Help a Brother Out

Mark 15:21

I revisited *Countering the Conspiracy to Kill Black Boys* by Dr. Jawanza Kunjufu, a book I had read some years ago. It gives advice to parents, educators, and church members for ensuring that African-American boys grow up to be strong, committed, and responsible African-American men. It answers questions such as, Is the future of African-American boys in the hands of their mothers and white female teachers? When does a boy become a man? Why are there more black boys in remedial and special education classes? The author says we must stop the dehumanization of African-American children. Could it be part of a conspiracy to kill black boys?

I raise this pivotal question today because years after the book was first published (which has been republished three times as of today), it appears eminently clear today that there is still a conspiracy to eradicate black men, and the prison system is the culprit. We've heard of two black men convicted of murder—Glenn Ford, who was in prison in Louisiana, and Edward Lee Elmore, who was imprisoned in South Carolina. Both were imprisoned for thirty years for crimes they had not committed, and Elmore had almost been executed three times, but thank God, their lawyers believed in them. Even though evidence was in their favor, they were convicted by all-white juries. Ford is sixty-four and Elmore is fifty-three. They spent half their lives in prison for crimes they had not committed, and since 1973, 144 death-row inmates have been cleared of crimes nationally, 10 in Louisiana alone.

It seems that black men have been taking the rap for years. We have been the scapegoat for years, and this is why I'm bothered when we start killing ourselves with black-on-black crime. Let's not kill each other but educate each other. Let's not kill each other but nurture each other. Let's not kill each other but fight for each other, for the law is against our young black boys as soon as they are born.

Even the Bible says that we are no longer under the law but under grace. So I say to all young black boys, get all the education you can because the world is afraid of an educated black man. When I think about black-on-black crime, I see two black men in this text: Simon of Cyrene, which is in north Africa, and Jesus, who from research was closer to being black than being of any other race. Revelation 1:14 says, "His head and hair were white like wool, as white as snow, and his eyes were like blazing fire." Here were two black men helping each other. They were minding their own business and doing good, but falsely accused Simon became a part of Jesus' supposed conspiracy.

Let me just propose today that all the brothers aren't bad. There are still some good men out there, and this brother comes to the rescue of another black man in distress. Who have you rescued lately?

Can you see this dramatic story unfolding in your mental skies today? Jesus' physical abuse was over. He had been beaten and bruised with a leather strap with pieces of sheep bones in it. Jesus was traveling slowly because the cross weighed about fifty pounds and his body was frail. Theologians have said that the cross was so heavy that it could have crushed the back of an ox, not to add the weight of sin. Remember that when Jesus carried the cross, he didn't carry the whole cross; he carried only the crossbeam, the *patibulum* that fit into the vertical bar already in the ground.

His enemies were anxious for him to carry his cross to the site of his execution, but they were afraid he might die before he got there. So they got someone else to carry the cross to "save" Jesus for his fate. Evil people never have good intentions. He was carrying that rough, heavy beam that was pressing into his lacerated skin and muscles. But thank

God, there was a man close by who was drafted to help Jesus carry his cross. He knew nothing about the impending crucifixion; he was just at the right place at right time, and he picked up Jesus' burden. Why? Because real men pick up each other's burden. We are there so another brother can lean on us. We all need somebody to lean on. Regardless of how heavy the situation is, the Lord will always send us some help, for according to Psalm 46, he is a very present help in times of trouble. Because Simon helped Jesus, he missed the opportunity to participate in the Passover and thus defiled himself.

Simon did not go there intending to help Jesus, but help found him. Simon was chosen just as Mary had been chosen to give birth to Jesus. The Lord does not always choose the known; sometimes, he chooses the unknown. He could have chosen Peter, James, or John, for they had been traveling with Jesus and listening to him for years, but everybody knew them.

When Jesus was ready to have his cross carried for him, he chose a stranger from Africa. God is not always going to raise up someone in the know. He won't always raise up a household name, or the most familiar church, or the person who pastors the biggest church. Every now and then, God will reach back and raise up someone you never heard of or seen before, like David, the little shepherd, or Mary Magdalene, who had seven demons cast out of her, or a prostitute named Rahab. Don't count me out just because you don't know me. The Lord knows my name.

As they forced Simon to carry Jesus' cross, something mystical happened that everyone missed. When Simon carried Jesus' cross, it placed Simon in Jesus' steps, and when we follow his footprints, we learn to walk like him. But we can't follow him without carrying what he carried. Jesus was walking before Simon, so it was impossible for Simon to carry the cross without following Jesus. This is why Jesus said in Luke 9:23, "Then he said to them all: If anyone would come after me, he must deny himself and take up his cross daily and follow me." We must carry the cross like Jesus, for it is meant to be carried, not dragged. Don't drag the cross, for that causes the cross to collect dust.

When we drag the cross, everything that the Lord came to deliver us from follows us. But when we carry it, we lift it.

Just as Jesus was prepared to conquer death, we need some brothers who are not afraid to help a brother carry his cross. Exodus 17:8–12 is a good story that illustrates this point. It's about the Amalekites, who attacked the Israelites. Moses said to Joshua, "Choose some of our men to fight, and tomorrow, I will stand on top of the hill with the staff of God in my hands." So Moses, Aaron, and Hur went to the top of the mountain, and as long as Moses held up his hands, Israel would prevail, but whenever he lowered his hands, the Amalekites seemed to be winning. When Moses' hands got tired, Aaron and Hur got a stone and put it under Moses, and those two brothers held up Moses' hands all day long.

That's what we need—brothers who will hold up each other's hands, for when our hands are up, we will win the war on drugs. When our hands are up, we will win the war against gang violence. When our hands are up, we win the war on crime. When our hands are up, we will win the war on poverty. Raise your hands!

Chapter 6

Where Are the Men?

Genesis 3:9

In 1971, Norman Whitfield and Barrett Strong of Motown wrote the song "Poppa Was a Rolling Stone." It became a remix in 1972, and was also sung by the Temptations. Some of the lyrics are as follows: "Poppa was a rolling stone. Wherever he laid his hat was his home, and when he died, all he left us was alone." More than forty years later, Poppa is still leaving his children alone. Why? It's because we're passing down to the next generation the vices and issues of the previous ones, and in some cases, we are doing what we saw our fathers do.

An African proverb says, "When we follow the path of our fathers, we learn to walk like them." We will walk like our role models. We can tell who a man is related to by the way he walks, and when we see young men walking around sagging, it means that they have started to mimic someone out of prison rather than out of college. Inmates aren't allowed belts in prison because they can be used as weapons, and to see so many young men doing this means they are preparing for prison instead of college.

But we can save our men. Save a man, save a seed; save a seed, save a family; save a family, save a generation. This goal can be accomplished, but right now, we are losing our men, especially in the African-American diasporas. The Bureau of Justice reports that 1 in every 15 African Americans is in prison and 1 in every 36 Hispanics is in prison as compared to 1 in every 106 white people. People of color make up 30 percent of the United

21

States population but account for 60 percent of the prison population. We are losing our men. This is why we're building more jails than colleges.

Let's see what Adam was doing in the text. Our story picks up immediately after the fall of man. Eve had been deceived by the snake, for that's what Satan is—a deceiver. So then, the effects of sin are punishment. They had life, but then they had death. They had pleasure, but then they learned about pain. Adam and Eve's first mistake was their sin, but their second mistake was trying to hide from God.

I want all men today to stop hiding. We must all step up to the plate and face our responsibilities. If we get women pregnant, we should commit to taking care of the child and send some child support to the mommas. We can never change what happened, but we can change the circumstance. We can change the lives of our children, and we can change the conditions our children have to grow up in. We can change our children's future if we stop hiding. Nobody should have to garnish our wages to get us to pay child support. Nobody should have to take us through the public humiliation of being on a talk show and taking a paternity test to see if a child is ours, and no child should have to grow up wondering who his or her daddy is. Stop hiding and face your responsibilities. Stop hiding behind your momma. You're an adult. The dilemma here in verse 8 lies in the fact that Adam believed he could hide from God. No, we can never hide from God.

We must get back to basics and implement what I call the three Ps of a man's faith: he should be priest, protector, and provider. As priests, we must become spiritual. As protectors, we must cover our households with prayer and take our families to church, temple, or mass. As providers, we must make sure our families have what they need. The first thing God told Adam after he was created was to get a job; in Genesis 2, he told him to cultivate the fields.

We need to affirm each other as men. Every twenty-eight days, women are affirmed in whom they are and how they were created; they are reminded of their femininity. But this is not the case with us men. We have nothing that specifically confirms our masculinity, so we must affirm each other; we must lift each other up. Every man needs someone to love him, and he needs someone to love.

Chapter 7

When Men Get Their Voices Back

Luke 1:57–66

The Christmas story tells us how important the man is in the family, the church, and the world, for when we scrutinize the story, we see how dominant the presence of men is, for it was a man in the person of an angel who announced to Elizabeth and Mary that they would have unusual births. The magi were men who traveled from Persia to Bethlehem to bring gifts to the baby Jesus. Shepherds, men, watched their flocks by night. All this indicates that God has always intended for men to a part of kingdom building.

The angel Gabriel represented the fact that men were called to announce the coming of a priest by the name of Jesus by making themselves the priests of their homes. The wise men represent that all men are to provide for their families just as the wise men provided gifts for Jesus. And the shepherds watching their flocks were symbolic of the fact that God has called men to be protectors and watchmen for their families.

All throughout the Christmas story, we see eminent illustrations of the roles of men as they relate to our duties and responsibilities as Christians. Something wonderful happens when men speak up, speak out, and get their voices back. Like Zechariah, we've lost them because of doubt and fear, and I ask, "Where are the voices of the men?" We see more women than men in our churches. The women are on the battlefield for the Lord while the men are on the golf course. We've lost our voices. More men are in prison than in college. We've lost our voices. We make babies but don't take care of them and become deadbeat dads. We've lost our voices. The presence of a father in the home is crucial to the nurturing and development of his children.

Even if we can't be in our children's homes, we can still be in their lives. But we have children today growing up not even knowing who their fathers are. Let me tell the sisters that if they have issues with the fathers, don't make those issues your children's issues, for when you do that, you will keep the fathers away from their children, especially if you don't tell them who their fathers are. When you do that, you are not turning the fathers away from the children, you are turning the children away from their mothers. The children will grow up hating somebody they have never met because all they hear about their father is negative things. If we are not careful, it could backfire.

I'm proposing today that we try to get as many men saved as we can, for when we save a man, we save a seed, and when we save a seed, we save a family. If we can save a family, we save a generation.

What makes this text so penetrating and far reaching is that it addresses the salvation of the father before the son could be introduced. We pick up the text after the angel has told Zechariah that he would be unable to speak because he had doubted the angel's announcement. Not only was he unable to speak, he was also unable to hear. He remained a deaf mute until the birth occurred. Well, in these verses, John the Baptist has arrived on the scene, and because Elizabeth had been in seclusion, the birth was a tremendous event in the neighborhood.

When it came time to name the child, everybody just assumed he would be named after his father, which was the Jewish tradition. But that would have meant that John the Baptist was coming only to prepare the Jews for Christ, when in fact he was coming to prepare the whole world for Christ.

I found two intriguing mysteries in this text. The first mystery is that Elizabeth, without prior knowledge of what her son's name would be, told everybody his name was going to be John. How did she know that? The angel didn't tell her, and Zechariah couldn't speak to tell her.

The second mystery is that when they asked Zechariah what his child's name would be, he confirmed what his wife said without hearing her, and he wrote the child's name on a tablet.

I see these mysteries and a warning notice that after the circumcision, they were going to name the child—they being the neighbors and relatives. Here's the warning: we need to be careful about letting other people name our children, for in many cases, if they name them, they will raise them, and there are some things that must stay with the parents.

The father got his voice back and said his name would be John. If Zechariah called his son John after he got his voice back, and if John was the forerunner of Jesus, then it's safe to assume that when we call another by a specific name, we get back whatever we lost. When we call the name of Jesus, we get back everything we lost. We can recover lost things just by calling his name. Sometimes, we go through too much paperwork trying to recover something when all we need to is call his name.

When we lose a job, just call his name, and another job, a better job with more benefits and pay will come our way. If we start losing our health, before we make appointments with our doctors, we should just call his name and healing will come to us. If we call his name, he will send what we lost, and we don't even have to tell him what we lost. The Bible says that at the name of Jesus, every knee shall bow and every tongue shall confess that Jesus is Lord. That's what happens when men get their voices back.

After he got his voice back and called out the name John, he went right into praise. He used the very thing he had lost to praise the Lord. We should learn to use what we have lost to give God praise. Often, we will lose something and wait for God to give it back to us. We will worship and praise the Lord and attend Bible study and prayer meeting. We will go to church weekly and start tithing because we are trying to get back what we lost, and that's fine, but that is just religion for the moment.

The problem is that we are not consistent. We ought to praise him after we lose something and praise him more after we get it back. That's what Zechariah did—he got his voice back. He used what he had lost to praise God more. He did not just kick up his heels when he got his voice back. No. He started giving God praise, and I imagine it was a different kind of praise. It was praise with a loud voice and excitement; he was starting to use his voice in ways he had never used it before.

What have you lost today? Have you found a way to honor and praise God with it? If you lost a car and God blesses you with another, do you give anybody a ride to church or do you just pass others by? There is a praise opportunity in giving others rides to church.

Zechariah was deaf and mute for nine months, but because of his faith, he got his voice back. This confirms for us that our droughts in life are just temporary setbacks. We all will experience sad days, and some are longer than others. Some rain will fall on all of us, but that rain won't last. The Lord uses our bad days to elevate us to our next levels of blessing. He takes us down only to lift us up; he caused us to go without so he will have the opportunity to provide for us. He causes us to go through the cold because it will be his opportunity to warm us up.

Zechariah almost missed out on his son's life.

Chapter 8

Anger Management

Genesis 4:3–12

Many of us remember the 1950s TV show *The Honeymooners*. Though I was not born until 1960, I used to watch reruns of the show. The show depicted Jackie Gleason as the overbearing Ralph Kramden who would rant and rave like a maniac while his wife, Alice, simply sat by and waited for his storms to pass. He would shake his fist in her face and tell her that she was going to the moon, but she never cowered in fear.

Ralph was a hothead who used anger as a tool, and whenever anger is used as a tool, it must be escalated to keep achieving any results. Ralph was a hothead, but he was fiction. One day, God told me there were men in our churches who were hotheads who had used their anger as a tool for so long that they had become anger addicts. We need to understand that if we cannot control our anger, we will become addicted to it. That's right—anger can be addictive just like drugs that give us a rush of adrenaline and feeling of invincibility. If people are intimidated by your outbursts and leap into action every time you blow up, then that can become like a drug to you.

Just as the Lord can deliver others from their addictions, he can deliver those who have anger management issues as well, but they must confess that to the Lord. A number of people in the Bible had problems with anger, including Moses, Samson, and Peter, but the person we want to focus on is Cain. Cain was a farmer, while Abel was

27

a shepherd. One day, Cain sacrificed and brought an offering from the ground, something he had planted and grown, but Abel sacrificed one of his best sheep to God. God smiled on Abel's but frowned on Cain's sacrifice because Cain's was a bloodless sacrifice and Abel's was a blood sacrifice, and without the shedding of blood, there can be no remission of sin, so Abel's sacrifice reminded God of redemption.

God will not accept some things we bring before him because like Cain's sacrifice, they will have been just thrown together—no forethought, no preparation or planning, just thrown together. Cain just grabbed something from the ground while Abel picked a fat sheep. Don't just throw something together and try to get by with it. Don't just throw a song together and call it worship. Don't just throw a worship service together and call it praise. Don't just put a few words together and call that a prayer. Don't just write a few words down and call them a sermon. No. Take time to be holy. That's why we need to be careful trying to acquire something just because somebody else has one. Someone buys a house, so we got to have one; someone buys a car, so we got to have one. But the difference is that person's home and car are anointed, and God has blessed him or her, but if we try to force a blessing on ourselves without allowing God to bless us in his time, it won't last.

So Cain had some issues. He was angry. In verse 6, God asked Cain, "Why are you so angry?" Now God realized Cain was angry and was about to do something stupid. He tried to caution him in verse 7, but Cain was angry because he had been rejected.

Many men have anger because they cannot handle rejection, which deflates their egos. Since they have never learned how to cope with deflated egos, they just follow them into their adulthoods. That's why there's so much violence in sports today. When a baseball player gets hit by a pitch, he wants to fight; when a basketball player gets fouled, he wants to fight. Why? Because that's an automatic response to rejection. They don't think of it as a bad pitch or an accidental elbow but as rejection: "You don't like me. You don't want to play with me." It ignites a fight. It may have started when they were young boys playing sports, and they have never learned to deal with it.

Men, we need to learn how to deal with rejection. If a sister is not interested in you, she is just not interested, but don't stalk her if she says no. Get over it. Meet somebody else.

God was unsuccessful in trying to get Cain to master his sin, which got the best of Cain. What we really need to understand is that his anger was not against Abel but against God. He couldn't kill God, so he killed his brother. Oh sons and daughters, what we have here is a transfer of anger. Many men who have anger management problems are those who have transferred their anger. Cain knew his arms were too short to box with God, so he took his anger out on his brother. A lot of men do that same thing. Some men are mad at their fathers because they had never spent time with them, never took them to baseball games, and never took them fishing. They've been mad at their earthly father for so long that they have transferred that anger to God. Now, they hate church and don't go and almost cuss you out whenever you mention church to them. It's because they blame God for everything, but God hasn't done anything to them. All he has done for them is to make a way out of no way.

After Cain killed Abel, God asked him where his brother was. "I don't know," Cain said. "Am I my brother's keeper?" He got an attitude with God. The answer is yes, we are our brothers' keepers. Yes, we are.

We must have our brothers' backs. Do you remember Exodus 17:12, when Moses told Joshua to go to war with Amalek and he did? Moses said he would lift up his arms, and when he did, Joshua would start being victorious, but when Moses lowered his tired arms, the Amalkites would start gaining the upper hand. Aaron and Hur helped Moses hold up his arms until the sun went down. Moses called that place Jehovah Nissi, which means "the Lord is our banner."

That's what it means to be our brothers' keepers. If one man gets on cocaine, every man should try to get him off it. If one brother has a problem with alcohol, every brother should get together and put him in AA. If one brother slips, another brother should pick him up. We must have each other's back. God calls us to help each other, not kill each other.

God told Cain that because of what he did, no crops would grow for him again. He told him that he thought he was rejected before, but after that, even the ground would reject him and he would become a restless wanderer, a vagabond, a beggar, all alone.

If we are not careful, men, our anger will leave us all alone. If you're single, you won't be able to get a date. If you're married, your wife will feel threatened and in some cases leave you. Your children will repudiate you, and nobody will want to be around you.

But in the quietness of your soul, if you just steal away to Jesus, he can and will remove the anger from your lives and replace hatred with love and a sweet spirit.

Chapter 9

A Memorial to Victory

Exodus 17:14–16

He became one of the most admired and adored athletes. He was a three-time world heavyweight boxing champion who finished his career with fifty-six wins, five losses, and thirty-seven knockouts. He was the only athlete to throw a gold medal into a river because of his disgust with racism. He was born Cassius Clay and later changed his name to Muhammad Ali.

Ali had a fighting style that he popularized in his 1974 "rumble in the jungle," his fight in Zaire with George Foreman. His fighting style was called rope-a-dope; he would assume a protective stance, lying against the ropes, and allow his opponent to hit him, oftentimes ducking and moving so that his opponent would hit air. His opponent would tire himself out and make mistakes, allowing Ali to explode in a counterattack.

God wants me to announce that today is the last day the enemy will take advantage of us, defy us, and beat up on us. God is using the rope-a-dope technique; he's allowing the enemy to tire himself out, make mistakes, and underestimate our ability and authority, for we are the ones Isaiah said would run and not get weary and walk and not faint. The enemy will become so tired of trying to bring us down and plotting and politicking against us that he will wear himself out and faint. Keep pressing on until the enemy is out for the count. We are over comers who will win the battle and the war.

Joshua was on the ground fighting the enemy with the sword while Moses was above him with his arms lifting a rod. We see from this biblical saga that we must be men and women of God who know how to fight and pray, for Joshua's sword was a symbol of war and Moses' rod was a symbol of prayer. The Amalekites, descendants of Esau, were a people whose name meant "warlike." They were well armed for battle, more so than Israel. The Amalekites knew the country, and they knew when to attack, and they attacked the Israelites when they were feeble, weak, tired, and suffering from thirst.

But the Lord still allowed the Israelites to achieve victory because they had something the Amalekites didn't see. They had a secret weapon, Jehovah, and whenever Israel went through something, Jehovah was always there, working behind the scenes to provide for them. He was so prevalent there that Moses called that place Jehovah Nissi, which means "the Lord is our banner." Jehovah is one of the Old Testament names for God, and it is translated in the Hebrew as Yahweh, which means "I am that I am" or "the one who is or causes to become." *Nissi* is Hebrew for "standard" or "banner." God was saying he would always be around to lift up and be our banner of defense.

Banners were important in the Bible because they were not only the focal point of war, they were also for the believers the focal point of victory. The Lord was so sure of victory that he said to Moses, "Write this on a scroll" as something to be remembered. Then Moses built an altar. The scroll represented the written word, and the altar represented a place of prayer and sacrifice.

We all need these two symbols of God's power in our homes and lives; we need the Word, and we need an altar. We are supposed to keep the Word in us, not on us. We have it on us now, on our phone, and on our iPad, and on the computer, and that's all right. But if our batteries get low, we're in trouble. The best place to keep the Word is in our hearts. David said in Psalm 119:105, "Your word is a lamp to my feet and a light for my path." We must keep it safe in our hearts.

And just as Moses built an altar, we all need a special place, a place set apart for meditation and prayer. Sometimes, we may need to make an emergency altar. Maybe the steering wheel when we're driving, or the hospital waiting room, but all of us need a place of prayer.

Look at what God said to Moses in the latter part of verse 14 about blotting out the memory of Amalek. Some things the Lord wants us to forget and some things he wants us to remember. We need to forget about the mistakes of our past, forget about those we loved but who abused us, forget about those things that used to keep us in bondage. For many of us, our minds are holding us hostage because we can't forget some things we need to forget. Come here, Paul. I hear him in Philippians: 3:13: "Forgetting what is behind and straining toward what is ahead I press on toward the goal to win the prize for which God has called me heavenward in Christ Jesus." There are some things you want to remember, however, such as how he set us free, how he brought us out, when he healed us and paid our bills for us with no job.

He said, "I will completely blot out the memory of Amalek." That was similar to what Moses said to Israel in Exodus 14:13: the Egyptians you see today you will never see again. That's what God is saying to Israel here. "I protected you from the Egyptians, I will protect you from the Amalekites, and you won't be bothered with them anymore." In other words, the Israelites weren't to raise a white flag in surrender; they were to raise a red flag because they were covered by God's blood.

We as well are not to surrender though we will have to fight many enemies. Israel was always fighting somebody because they were God's chosen people. Chosen people are blessed people, and as such, they always have to fight off somebody trying to steal from them. Blessed people always have to fight to protect God's property, but they will not surrender to gangs, drugs, and alcohol; they will surrender only to the one they are covered by. All to Jesus I surrender!

Moses called that place of memorial and victory Jehovah Nissi. The best way to remember some spiritual and historical events is by giving them names. When God provided Abraham and Sarah with Isaac, they laughed at God first, but when Isaac was born, they named him Isaac, which means "laughter." When the Lord provided the ram for

Abraham in Genesis 22, he called that place Jehovah Jireh, "the Lord will provide." When Moses was drawn from the Nile, he was named Moses, which means "drawn out of."

If at times in your life the Lord did something miraculous, give it a name. If the operating room is where you experienced his healing hand, call that room your miracle room, and every time you visit that hospital, walk by the room and say, "That's my miracle room." Take a picture of the car you wrecked in an accident that you walked away from. Call it "from wreck to praise," and if you ever want to know how good God has been, just look at that photo and praise him.

This text is about the Lord fighting for us. The battle is not ours; it is the Lord's. Sometimes, when the Lord fights for us, he won't destroy all our enemies; he will keep some around because he wants them to see us rise, and he wants them to see us bounce back. That's why Psalm 23 says he prepares a table for me in the presence of my enemies.

Chapter 10

I Want You Back

Judges 16:22–30

We were all shocked to hear about Rachel Canning, that teenager who attempted to sue her parents because they had asked her to leave their home due to her not wanting to abide by their rules dealing with curfew, chores, and dating. They told her that if she was going to live in their house, she would have to end a relationship with a guy they felt was a bad influence on her. She refused. She decided to leave.

The teenager was seeking $650 a week in child support, tuition at her high school, and attorney's fees. The judge denied the case, stating that it could lead down a slippery slope of claims against parents.

The real tragedy was that these kinds of acrimonious actions could destroy the sacred relationship between parents and children. This child didn't understand that she needed her parents more than her parents needed her. The reason she was not remorseful was that even when she left, she started staying with a friend. She was too comfortable to learn any lesson because she was spoiled. She thought she could get whatever she wanted just by asking, not by working.

This was when her parents should have applied the psychology of the posterior and support by Scripture and say to her that the Bible said that whom the Lord loves he chastises. They should have told her that what they were going to do would hurt them more than her, but they'd do it anyway because they loved her. "Go get a switch. If you can't find a switch, bring me anything." Then they should have let her leave. After being on the streets with no money, no food, no clothes, that child would be saying, "Mommy and Daddy, I want you back!"

The Lord will always receive us back because he wants us back. That's why in the parable of the lost sheep in Luke 15, he left ninety-nine sheep to look for one. Isn't it good news that the Lord takes us back even after we've been in the world? He takes us back after we have been pigs and have spent all our money on the fast life.

We find Samson in this text at a time in his life when he had lost a lot. He lost his eyes, strength, hair, the woman who became a mole for the enemy, and the woman he was in love with but wasn't in love with him. Most important, he lost his anointing.

He lost all that because of his obsession with women. Sexual addictions and perverted escapades are often the culprits that bring down powerful leaders. Bill Clinton was the second U.S. president to be impeached (the first was Andrew Johnson), and it all started over a blue dress. A few years ago, former South Carolina governor Mark Sanford went missing in action. No one knew where he was; he had told his office he was on a hiking trip. Turns out he went to Argentina to be with his mistress whom he later married, causing him to forfeit his political career, his wife, and four sons. Even in the Bible, we see this kind of scandalous propensity when King David had a woman's husband killed so he could be with her. Solomon was known as the wisest man in the Bible, but he had 700 wives and 300 concubines.

This Scripture confirms two pivotal issues. Satan not only attacks our weaknesses, he also attacks our strengths. Samson's weakness was women, and his strength was his anointing (hair). I see something else that is disturbing to me in this text: the Philistines praised their god after Samson, their enemy, was captured. They praised Dagon, an idol represented as man and fish. From the navel down he was a fish, and from his navel up he was a man. The Philistines were fisherman, and they believed that the worship of Dagon would bless them with more fish. We read about Dagon in 1 Samuel 5; the Philistines took the ark of the covenant to Dagon, and every time Dagon was in God's presence, he fell to his face and lost his head, for idols and their worship cannot stand before a divine God.

This god received all the Philistines' praise. The problem was that they had put a lot of planning, ingenuity, and orchestration into praising the wrong god. Don't let the wrong crowd praise their god more than we praise ours. More important, when we spend millions a year on pot in Colorado but won't give anything to our churches, we are praising the wrong God. When Massachusetts legalized the right of men to take up-skirt pictures of women, when Florida used its stand-your-ground law to justify the killing of innocent black boys, then we are praising the Devil. Don't worship him more and louder than we worship the true, living God.

Samson became a prisoner of the Philistines. They tortured him, and he lost his eyesight. They made a mistake, however; they left his hands. In verse 26, he asked the servant leading him by his hand to put him where he could feel the pillars. He was able to use what he had left. I don't care what the enemy strips us of. I don't care how devastating it was, we can use what we have left to fight with, and God will add to it because he can do more with leftovers than the enemy can do with what he took from us.

Hezekiah was sick, but God added fifteen years to his life. He added twelve baskets to five loaves and two fishes. If we have a left hand, God will add one of his hands to that one. If we have just one foot left, God will add one his feet. If we have just one eye left, God will give us one of his. We should not become depressed about what the enemy took; we should just praise God for what we still have—hope, determination, and brains. There ain't no harm in keeping our minds on Jesus. That's why Isaiah said he would keep us in perfect peace those whose minds were stayed on him.

Samson wanted to feel the pillars. He wanted to be in the right position before he could be used by God. Position yourself for a blessing. Some are wondering why they are here, why they had to move across country, why they couldn't have just stayed in the position they were in. We must understand that there is something called divine providence; the Lord has us where he wants and needs us. If the Israelites had not gone to Egypt, they would have never experienced the miracle at the Red Sea. If they had not experienced that, they would not have had their experience in the wilderness. If it weren't for the wilderness, they would not have experienced the Promised Land.

If David had never had the opportunity of being a shepherd, he would have never been able to say that the Lord was my shepherd, I shall not want. If Zaccheus had not been in the sycamore tree, he would have missed Jesus. If Bartimaeus had not been on the Jericho road, he would have never received his sight. If the woman at the well had not been positioned there, she would have never met Jesus. Are you in your position?

Samson felt humiliated; the Philistines did not see him as a threat. He was no longer viewed as the undefeated, indisputable judge of Israel, and they forced him to dance and parade like a clown. But they took him for granted. They started celebrating too soon.

In verse 28, Samson prayed and repented because he knew he had messed up. He asked the Lord to give him his glory back just one time. (I want you back.) The Lord heard him and redeemed him and restored him. Samson brought the house down.

That's the article—bring the house down. God needs men who will bring the dope houses down, the gangs' houses down, the crack houses down, the pimps' and prostitutes' houses down, bring political corruption down, and bring the house of racism down.

Don't you see that the house killed the enemies when the house was right with God, right with glory, right with fellowship? Then, all those who are unholy or who have hidden agendas will be able to enter the house. They will walk in, but they will have to leave immediately.

Samson got his spirit right, and with the right spirit, he brought the house down on himself and his enemies. It was not a suicide mission; it was a mission of fulfillment. He died fulfilling his mission, which was to save Israel. Greater love has no man than to lay down his life for his friends.

Chapter 11

Mistakes of a Biblical Superman

Judges 14:1–4, 15:1, 16:1–5

All of us remember Superman on TV. He was born with superhuman strength. He was able to leap tall buildings with a single bound. He was more powerful than a locomotive. He was faster than a speeding bullet, and whenever trouble would raise its ugly head, he would go into a telephone booth or a back office somewhere and change his clothes, break out into a cape, and soar through the air. The crowds would say, "Look up in the air! It's a bird. No, it's a plane. No, it's Superman!"

He would save people from crime and danger, and even though he was a strong man, he had two secrets. The first secret was that he hid behind the façade of a newspaper journalist named Clark Kent. Some men are like that; they hide behind façades so no one can see who they really are. They hide behind baggage from their pasts or fake personalities. They pretend to be educators by day but are on the prowl by night.

Superman's other secret was that he was vulnerable to kryptonite, something that could drain all his strength. Men, we need to come to grips with our weaknesses. We all have weaknesses, but if we pray and fast and trust God, we can overcome them. Paul did, and that's why in 2 Corinthians 12:10, Paul said, "I take pleasure in my infirmities, necessities, my reproaches, and my persecutions for when I am weak then am I strong." David, after he had succumbed to a moment of weakness, said in Psalm 51:7, "Purge me with Hyssop and I shall be clean, wash me and I shall be whiter than snow!"

Weaknesses lead to mistakes, and as men of God, we can overcome our weaknesses and learn valuable lessons from our mistakes.

This brings us to our text. We find in the text a biblical superman by the name of Samson, indeed somewhat of a Hebrew Hercules. He had enormous strength. He was a giant and a gymnast. He was so strong that he killed a lion with his bare hands. He killed a thousand men with the jawbone of a jackass, broke ropes and cords that bound him, and carried the gate of a city called Gaza by himself. He was strong because God had made him that way.

After the generation of Joshua had died out, there was no king in Israel, so every man was on his own. There was no central government, and Israel was under the Philistines for forty years. God needed to raise up someone who could defeat the Philistines, and at that time, an angel visited an elderly couple. The husband's name was Manoah. His wife was sterile. The angel appeared to her and told her that she was going to conceive and was going to bear a son but that he was going to be raised in the tradition of a Nazirite, which meant he could not drink strong drink, he had to abstain from certain things, he couldn't go near dead bodies, and he wasn't allowed to cut his hair because Nazirites were to be separated from the world and consecrated to God.

Only three Nazirites were mentioned in the Bible: Samson, Samuel, and John the Baptist. Samson, however, like superman, had a secret. All his strength was in his hair, which was the only visible sign he had been separated and consecrated.

We ought to have some tangible signs that we have been consecrated by God—a song, a prayer, a lifestyle, something! Samson had been consecrated by God. He was the strongest man in the Bible, but even though he was physically strong, he still had some weaknesses. He still made mistakes, and he still had issues.

Let's see if we can find his mistakes in chapter 14:1–4. He saw a Philistine woman in Timnah and instantly wanted to marry her. He didn't know anything about her but he wanted to marry her because she looked good. He did this with two factors against him. First, she was a

Philistine, and the Philistines ruled Israel, so she was the enemy. Second, his parents objected. Samson wanted to hook up with the woman because she looked good, and he wanted to use her to get to the enemy.

Men, we should never hook up with women for the wrong reasons. If we do, it will come back to haunt us, and in Samson's case, it did. This woman allowed herself to be used by the other Philistines to get Samson to tell them the answer to the riddle. He told the people a riddle and said they had seven days to figure it out. If they did, he would give them some fine clothes. If not, then they would have to give him some fine clothes.

They pressed his wife for the answer, and her loyalty was to her people, not Samson. She cried to Samson in verse 15 that he didn't love her because he wouldn't give her the answer to the riddle. She cried for seven days before he finally told her the answer. She told her people, and as a result, a fight started between Samson and the people because the woman he had wanted to marry had betrayed him. Her loyalties were not to Samson.

Every time we marry or want to marry for the wrong reason, somebody is going to get betrayed. You can't marry someone just because he has money; you can't marry someone just because she's fine, because sooner or later, he will run out of money and she will get old one day. The only thing that will to keep you together is love, which is patient, kind, long suffering, and not easily puffed up. Take time to fall in love, and then get married.

In 15:1, we find this biblical superman's second mistake. It would seem that after she had nagged him for the answer to the riddle, Samson would have realized she was not the one for him. But not Samson. He wanted to go back to her and patch things up not with flowers or chocolates but with a goat. We must be careful that we don't get burned by the same man or woman twice. Learn your lesson the first time. But men, we keep going back because we're so afraid we won't be able to get anybody else. Maybe somebody told us we would never be anything in life, that maybe we were too fat or had too many kids. And we've been carrying around that emotional baggage for so long that we have started to believe it, so we keep going back to the same old mental abuse and allowing the same person to run the same old game on us because we don't think we could ever meet anybody else. The devil is a liar.

After Samson tried to go back to his wife, look at what he did in 16:1 and 4. He slept with a prostitute and fell in love with another woman, Delilah. Both of these women betrayed him. Samson had a problem with women and had no self-control. His weakness becomes another's strength. That's the thing, men. If we don't ask God to give us self-control, others will use our kindness as weakness.

As big as Samson was, as strong as he was, he was not strong enough to resist women. Just in this text we see him with three different women, and all of them used him. Delilah had Samson wrapped around her finger. He told her the secret to his strength, and the Scripture says that she put him to sleep on her lap. Samson didn't have any self-control. He loved women too much. There is nothing wrong with loving women, just one at a time.

After he went to sleep, she had someone shave his head. His strength left. His eyes were gouged out, and he was put in prison with bronze shackles. He was made to dance for them to entertain them.

Here is the point I want you to get. Samson said to the servant who was leading him, "Put me where I can feel the temple pillars." In verse 28, Samson prayed: "Lord, remember me O God. Strengthen me just once more and let me with one blow get revenge on the Philistines." God heard his prayer. He pushed, the pillars tumbled, and everyone was killed. His prayer came too late. The prayer he prayed was the one he should have prayed when he was fooling around with all those women. His prayer came at the end of his life, but it should have come at the beginning of his life.

Chapter 12

When the Missing Is Not Missed

Judges 16:20b

The business world maxim is that you have to change or die. This was true for Kodak, a company founded in 1888 by George Eastman. For almost a century, the name Kodak was synonymous with film. The company turned photography into a mass hobby with its $1 brownie camera and ultimately became a company worth over $2 billion.

But with the advent of digital photography, film became a thing of the past. Because Kodak could not keep up with the digital world, Kodak filed for bankruptcy in 2012. When we become oblivious to the change occurring around us, we become comfortable and complacent—and we become bankrupt.

Bankrupt Christians are those who have operated on their own merit, knowledge, ingenuity, and skills for so long that when the very thing that validates and empowers them is gone, they don't even miss it because they have been singing Frank Sinatra's "I did it my way" for so long that they believe it. But our ways will make us broke, will take us to hell, and will cause us to forfeit the power that comes from God. With no power, we can no longer stand on his promises but we end up sitting on his premises.

Israel was in a desperate need of deliverance from the Philistines, and Samson would do that. He enjoyed a singular privilege afforded to only one other person in the Old Testament. His birth was foretold to his parents by an angel, just as Isaac was promised to Abraham and Sarah by angels. The angel of the Lord promised Manoah and his wife that they would have a son dedicated to God who was to be a lifelong Nazirite. He was going to be empowered by God with supernatural strength. Samson was so strong that whenever the Spirit of God moved upon him, he could do unimaginable things. He caught 300 foxes, tied their tails together in pairs, set a torch to them, and caused them to destroy a vineyard and city. He once killed 1,000 Philistines with the jawbone of an ass. He ripped apart a lion with his bare hands. He even carried the gates of Gaza upon his back. In each instance, the Spirit of the Lord was upon him.

Even though he was strong, he is not remembered for his great exploits and victories but for his fall; he relinquished his anointing for the love of an adulterous woman.

Samson had a weakness for women. He married someone from Timnah, then he slept with a prostitute in Gaza, then he fell in love with Delilah. All of them, especially Delilah, were snares of the enemy. She was hired by the Philistines to discover the secret of his strength. He told her that the secret of his strength and consecration was in his hair. We need to keep some secrets to ourselves; if they get out, they can cause us public embarrassment. We should tell our secrets to God, who knows how to keep a secret. Psalm 90:8 says he keeps our secret sins in the light of his own countenance.

Once Delilah discovered where his strength was, she arranged to have his hair cut. When he got up to fight, his strength was gone. Verse 20 says he did not know that the Lord had left him. His anointed power was missing, and he did not know it had gone because his passion for women had replaced his passion for God, which nobody should ever let go of. He had started walking in the flesh; that's when lust leaves the heart exposed. This is why Proverbs 4:23 says, "Above all else, guard your heart, for it is the wellspring of life." We need to guard our heart because everything we do flows from it.

Delilah controlled him; she had his heart under siege, and he told her everything she wanted to know. Proverbs 7:21–22 tells us, "She seduced him with her smooth talk all at once he followed her like an ox going to the slaughter." Brothers, we need to watch who we get tangled up with just because they look good—it might be a setup. They will slaughter our reputations, slaughter our marriages, slaughter our money, and slaughter our relationships with our children.

In verse 20, we learn that Samson had been asleep when his hair was cut. That's right when he should have been awake. Remember what Jesus said to his disciples in Matthew 26:40 when he returned from the garden of Gethsemane and found them sleeping: "Could you not keep watch with me for one hour?" Samson became so comfortable with her that he was sleeping with the enemy but didn't know it. Delilah's name means "devotee," but she was not devoted to Samson; she was devoted to the Philistines who had hired her. She was working undercover.

We have to make sure that those who are interested in us are interested because they genuinely care about us. If not, then when we fall in love with them, we fall in love with everybody they are working for, and everybody is all of a sudden in our business. Genuine love keeps outsiders out. This is the issue with affairs. When married people have affairs, everybody they have been with comes into their bedrooms and into their business.

Here is the most profound verses in this Scripture; Samson didn't know the Lord had left him. His anointing had left, and he didn't even miss it. When we get so comfortable and confident with our accomplishments and successes, we forget about God, and according to Romans 12:3, we start thinking more highly of ourselves than we ought, and we don't miss what we had. Then questions arise: Did we ever have it? Was it ever ours in the first place? Samson lost the glory of God and had no knowledge of it. I can't speak for anybody else, but I need his glory. I can't do anything without it. We cannot sing without his glory, we cannot preach without his glory, and we cannot serve without his glory. It's a cataclysmic tragedy for the church to be without glory and to become immune to it; that means we never really experienced God's glory.

The reason we don't even recognize in church that the glory is gone is because we know what we are going to do before we get there. We don't make any room for the glory to show up. Everything is staged.

We praise on cue, we shout on cue, we dance on cue, and we get happy on cue because the worship service is staged.

But when God comes, he doesn't make an announcement, he doesn't RSVP, he never calls ahead; he just shows up and changes the order of service so that it operates around him, not us. That's because it's not about us but about him.

Chapter 13

Filling Empty Seats

1 Samuel 20:18

Dr. Bill Cosby and Dr. Alvin Poussaint wrote *Come on, People,* a book about the path from victims to victors. The book covers many areas, such as reclaiming our communities and streets and getting a good education. But the authors spend much time talking about the plight of African-American men—their absence in their homes and in their children's lives, especially their sons' lives.

The authors share interesting statistics: 70 percent of our babies are born to single women; the divorce rate among black people is 60 percent. Of the 16,000 homicides committed in this country each year, more than half are committed by black men. In some cities, black men have a high school dropout rate of more than 50 percent. Black men make up 12 percent of the general population but constitute 44 percent of the prison population. One in four young black men is in the criminal justice system, and about 33 percent of the homeless are black men.

It is amazing what the presence of fathers can do in the lives of their children, especially boys. Children don't ask for their fathers' résumés, or references, or bank account statements; they just want their fathers in their lives. And if their fathers can make that commitment, no matter how hopeless or useless fathers may think they are, they will be much better men than they thought they were. This is what Bill Cosby and Alvin Poussaint say in *Come on, People*.

But this is what I say. Homes without fathers are homes with empty seats. For there is no head at the table, no priest in the home, no protector for the home, and it all falls on the shoulders of the mother. Let us give a huge shout-out to all the single mothers in our homes and churches who did it God's way. Let us give a huge shout-out to all the fathers who love their children, take care of their children, pay child support, and will always be in their lives.

Our text, about the relationship between Jonathan and David, is concise but gripping. Jonathan's father, Saul, did not like David; he was jealous of him and wanted to kill him, but Jonathan and David were good friends, and the preceding verse says that he loved him as he loved himself, and they made a covenant (God as witness) with each other that they would take care of each other and each other's households. So thick was this bond between David and Jonathan that they even arranged for Jonathan to communicate to David his father's scheme to kill him using arrows (verses 18–20). This brief text discusses how Jonathan would let David know what Saul's state of mind was. When he spoke about the seat being empty, he was confirming what David said about hiding in the field in verse 5.

The new moon festival was a time of feasting on rams and bulls, when sinners received atonement and were reconciled with the Lord. It represented a time of fellowship; it was like a family dinner, and it has been proven that when children have family dinners, they do better in school.

But this says something else to me. If the new moon represents a time of feasting for reconciliation, it is also for me a sign of provision, and when the man of the house is absent from the dinner table, spiritual provision is also absent. An empty seat is indicative of a man's inability to provide for his family's spiritual needs.

As men, we are called to take care of our families, not just financially but also spiritually. It's our job to lead our families in prayer, to take them to church, to expose them to a spiritual environment, and anoint our houses with oil. We must provide for our children as the Lord provides for us, for he is our Jehovah Jireh—he will provide for us.

Although this text is concise, it says something about empty seats. This is the premise, and it's not gender bias. We need to be careful whom we allow to fill the empty seats of our homes. We need to be careful whom we allow in our homes, around our children, and sitting at our tables.

We shouldn't be so quick to fill Daddy's or Mommy's shoes. We shouldn't be so quick to let people we barely know into our spaces. What took months and years to establish can be eradicated in a matter of minutes if the wrong spirit is invited in. Stop falling in love with someone overnight, and stop talking about marriage after the first date. Make sure that they are not on America's Most Wanted list; if America wants them, you don't. If that means we have a seat remain empty for a little longer, so be it, for filling it too quickly could bring disaster.

Everything Saul was trying to do to David was really a decoy by the enemy to preclude David from becoming the new king of Israel. It was already in God's will that David would become the next king (read the next three chapters of the Bible and you will discover this), so when we read that our seats will be empty, I want us to think as though the king-elect seat is empty, and here is when the king's seat is empty. The church is vulnerable to attack. We need to make sure that our King, the Lord, has a seat in the church, for Jesus is the head of the church, and if he doesn't have a seat, the church is vulnerable to attack. The choir can sing like angels, but it means nothing if the King is not present. The sermons may be prepared adequately, but they mean nothing if the King is not present. Our churches can have beautiful pews and wonderful stained glass windows, but if the King is not present, they don't mean anything.

There is more hell in the church than heaven and more demons than angels because we are under attack due to the fact that the King is not there. Why? Because he had never been invited. How many times do we send out invitations about our church programs but forget to invite the Lord?

Holy Spirit, you are welcome in this place. You are welcome to move, save, anoint, and have your way.

Chapter 14

Lean on Me

Exodus 17:11–12

How important is church to us? Do we go out of commitment or guilt? Brotherhood and sisterhood or livelihood? If we want to know how important church is to us, we should pay close attention to what we have allowed the church to become for us. If we go to church but just play on our iPads and iPhones, that means church is nothing more than a game for us. If we start clipping our fingernails in church, it becomes nothing more than a manicurist's shop to us. If we go to church only when it is our Sunday to serve rather than coming each Sunday, that means that the church is just our part-time love and that we flirt with God rather than loving him with all our heart, mind, and soul. If we go to church only when we are going through something, that means we are using God, playing him instead of serving him. If we do any of these things, that means we lean on them instead of leaning on God, and superficiality will not get us through.

In 1972, Bill Withers understood this and penned the lyrics to the song "Lean on Me": "Lean on me when you're not strong, and I'll be your friend. I'll help you carry on, for it won't be long till I'm gonna need somebody to lean on." We all need somebody to lean on, and his name is Jesus. Solomon reaffirmed the song; he put a spiritual connotation on it and said in Proverbs 3:5, "Trust in the Lord with all

50

thine heart, and lean not unto thine own understanding but in all thy ways acknowledge him and he will direct thy path."

In one region of Africa, Christians were very diligent about praying. Believers had their own special places outside the village where they would pray. They would use private footpaths through the brush to reach their individual prayer rooms. When grass started to grow over this or that path, it was evident who was not praying. Whenever someone noticed an overgrown prayer path, he or she would go to the person whose path it was and say, "Brother [or sister], there's grass on your path. We need to lean on the one who knows how to keep our paths clean of weeds, undesirables, and evil influences."

This text affirms God as Jehovah Nissi, which means "the Lord is our banner" or "the Lord fights for us," for here we find Moses in the middle of a battle with the Amalekites, Israel's longtime enemy. These descendants of Esau were nomads in the desert south of Canaan. They were attempting to dislodge Israel and to bask in the oasis of the land. But God was angry with them because they refused to recognize the hand of God in Israel's life and destiny and would attack Israel's sick, elderly, and anyone who lagged behind, according to Deuteronomy 25. They didn't fight fair.

Moses called on Joshua to galvanize an army to fight against the Amalekites while Moses would raise high the staff of God. This staff symbolized Israel's total dependence not on Moses but on the power behind the staff. This was the same staff Moses used to turn water into blood and that turned into a cobra once. Joshua's sword and Moses' staff were to be in operation simultaneously.

As long as Moses' hands were lifted, Joshua and his men appeared to be winning. But when Moses' hands were lowered because of fatigue, the Amalekites would start winning. So Aaron and Hur (tradition says that this was the husband of Moses' sister Miriam) literally held up Moses' hands, which his troops interpreted as Moses asking God for victory, and this inspired them.

That's the same thing Jesus was doing for us when his arms were stretched for us from the cross; he was pleading our case for us. Sometimes, before we give up, before we call it quits, before we resign, before we think about change, we need to lift our hands and say, "Father, I stretch my hand to thee!"

Notice that Moses' hands were getting tired in verse 12, and this prompted Aaron and Hur to get a stone and sit Moses on it. This stone or rock has an interesting interpretation in Exodus 17:1–7. When the Israelites were in the desert and were thirsty, they complained about it to Moses, and God said, "Moses, strike the Rock." He did, and water came out, reminiscent of John 7:38: "Out of his belly shall flow rivers of living water." But then in 1 Corinthians 10:4, we learn that the rock was Christ, so when Moses sat on it, he got his second wind.

Jesus Christ will give us all our second winds. No wonder he said to us in Matthew 11:28, "Come unto me all ye that labor and are heavy laden and I will give you rest." Some men have been leaning on the wrong things for a second wind, and all of those things will just make them that much more tired. They have been running from their responsibilities to provide child support, being the men of their homes, raising their children, and working hard. It's high time for them to sit on a rock.

After Moses sat on the rock in verse 12, Aaron and Hur held his arms up until sunset, a long time, so that the Israelites' fortunes in the battle would stop fluctuating. Today, we may be on top of the world, but tomorrow, we could be in the pit. Today, we may be employed, but tomorrow, we could be receiving unemployment. Today, we may be well, but tomorrow, we could be sick. Today successful—tomorrow bankrupt. God takes us through these times to remind us not to trust in riches or fame but to trust in the one who holds tomorrow. We should know that if God clothes the lilies, feeds the birds, and shelters the foxes, he will take care of us.

If we aren't careful, we will miss the hidden revelations in the text, and this is one. At first glance, it appeared to me that Aaron and Hur were holding up Moses, but I looked again, and it then appeared to me that Moses was holding them up. They were holding him up physically, but he was holding them up with spiritual strength. Physical strength does not make men strong—spiritual strength does that. And Moses was strong spiritually. He had the rock, which represented Christ. He had the rod, which represented power. His hands were lifted, which represented his ability to stand in the gap for them.

On Fathers' Day, just like on every day, we need fathers who are strong not because of what they can bench press but strong in Christ. That's why we read in Mark 3:7, "No one can enter into a strong man's house and steal his goods without binding him first." That passage is talking about strong in the Word, strong in the anointing, strong in prayer.

One commercial I saw tries to demonstrate the safety of Subarus. It shows a tow truck driver dragging mangled Subarus to the junkyard. One by one, the drivers of those cars look at their wrecks and realize how lucky they were to be alive, to have survived their crashes. It is not a car that keeps us alive but someone we have learned to lean on, someone safer than any Subaru. He is our seat belt, he is our air bag, he is our safety net. If we just lean on him, he will hold us up.

Chapter 15

A Father's Response to a Son's Request

Luke 11:11–13

A little boy followed exactly in his father's footsteps through a new garden. He said, "Daddy, if you don't get mud on your feet, I won't get mud on mine." I want every father to think about that. If our children want to be just like us, what kind of adults would they grow up to be?

That's a poignant question, especially when we think about some of the findings that Ronald Sider made in his book, *The Scandal of the Evangelical Conscience: Why Are Christians Living Just Like the World?* He stated that there have been many polls taken by noted Christian researchers such as the Gallop Organization and the Barna Group that has found that every day, the church is becoming more like the world it allegedly seeks to change. They state that Christian men beat their wives as often as their unsaved neighbors do, that Christians are just as materialistic and racist as their pagan friends, and that there is just as much scandalous behavior in the church as there is in the world. These polls found that some Christians commit treason every day with their mouths because they claim Jesus is Lord, but their actions demonstrate their allegiances to money, sex, and self-fulfillment.

Many of our young people are not really sure of what they want to become because who and what they thought they wanted to do has disappointed, confused, and astonished them. They wanted to be police officers until they saw a policeman involved in police brutality. They had hopes of becoming teachers until they saw a teacher involved in molestation. They felt the call to the ministry until they read about a priest or a pastor getting involved in heinous crimes. They don't know what they want to do now.

Fathers, we are our children's last resort. We need to live in such a way that our children will say, "I want to be just like my daddy. He doesn't have a big title or a lot of education or money, but he had character and integrity."

In this text, we find Jesus teaching two parables. In the first one, in verses 5–8, he taught about prayer. He presented himself as our heavenly Father giving us what is good for us. He introduced us to a son asking his father for something. The father would never give his child something that would harm him; he wouldn't give him a snake if he asked for a fish or wouldn't give him a scorpion if he asked for an egg. Today, some fish, such as eels, resemble snakes, and a large white scorpion when it's all rolled up could resemble an egg. But the father who has made all things knows the difference even if the son is sometimes too naïve to understand.

In this parable, Jesus used the fish and the scorpion. Remember that in Luke 9:16, he took two pieces of fish and five loaves of bread and fed a multitude. In Luke 10:19, he said to his disciples, "Behold I have given you authority to trample on snakes and scorpions and over all the power of the enemy and nothing shall harm you." This represents the fact that God always gives us more than enough. The snakes and scorpions represent the obstacles we must overcome; this means that our Father will never give us something that looks like something else. Our heavenly Father does not give us look-alikes, but for too long, we have been looking spiritual while living like heathens; we have been pretending to be faithful but we have really been on the prowl. We have been pretending that we are happy but we are really miserable. Our Father, however, is consistent.

We cannot be imitation fathers, for there is nothing like the real thing. Computers are raising our children. Everything they want to know they can get from computer games, cell phones, and the TV. These media have become the surrogate, proxy, and illegitimate parents of many of our children. At one time, sending a child to his or her room was used as discipline, but now they have so much in their rooms that such punishment is more recreation than discipline. Our children spend more time with gadgets than they do with guidance from us, more time on Facebook than they do having conversations with us face to face. And we, the parents, spend more time on Facebook than we do in the face of God, seeking his direction.

We are raising a generation of young people we don't really know, and the longer our children are on the computer, the more time the enemy, who comes in the form of a cyberspace demon, can speak to them in chat rooms. So they chat with the enemy instead of us because they have been ensnared. These kinds of technological gimmicks should not raise our children for us. There is nothing like loving parents. Technology can't hold them and comfort them when they need that. It can't protect them or teach them how to ride a bike, fish, and behave properly. Psalm 127:3 says that children are a reward from God, so we must nurture our reward.

Then notice the twist in the text; the Lord called the fathers evil. If you are evil but still give gifts, then realize that the Lord, who is sinless, can do even more. The text is pointing out that we are all sinners saved by grace. All of us have been bad children, but God is a good God for bad children. All of us have messed up. No matter how successful we are today, no matter how respected we are today, we all live in haunted houses, and if we glide through life unrepentant and unremorseful, one day, a ghost from our past will arise at the most inopportune time. Life, when it is lived right, has a way of keeping us humble, and the Holy Spirit will always remind us that we are sinners saved by grace.

In the end, the Holy Spirit is all we have to give our children, but that is the best gift a father and mother could give a child. He will guide them, he will speak to them, and he will keep them.

After moving to a new neighborhood, a little girl got lost walking to the park. A policeman asked her what was wrong. She said, "I'm lost, we don't have a phone, yet, and I don't know my new address yet." He said, "Well, is there a landmark by your house?" She said no, but then she thought about it. She said, "There's a cross next to my father's house, and if I can make it to the cross, I believe I can find my way back home."

Chapter 16

Without a Trace

2 Samuel 13:38, 14:28

It used to be that when a little boy was asked what he wanted to be, he would say he wanted to be just like his daddy; he wanted to be a policeman like his daddy, or a fireman like his daddy. Now, however, we live in a fatherless generation, a time when our young boys have very few role models because there is a tremendous absence of men in our homes. Forty percent of the households in this country have no father at home, and between 60 and 70 percent of all African-American homes have no father. That translates into homes in which mothers are raising boys, and so the boys' first examples are their mothers, which can lead to future problems if those young boys aren't exposed to masculine personalities.

We all have to come to grips with this problem and combat it. The absence of a father in the home affects girls and boys. Girls are getting pregnant because there is no man at home to authenticate them and to tell them how pretty they are and how wonderful they are. They contend with this by getting pregnant so they can do for their babies what their fathers didn't do for them. They hug their babies because their fathers didn't hug them. They take time with their children because their fathers didn't take time with them. This fatherless generation affects girls as well.

Boys are affected by the absence of a father; that can lead them into relationships with girls, get them pregnant, and then leave because that's what their fathers did to their mothers. We have teenage boys who have never seen their fathers, so they get involved in gangs and make them their families, their fathers. We have some serious issues that we must deal with, and many of them are a result of this fatherless syndrome. Thank God for blended families, for it gives young boys opportunities to have relationships with men.

I know of no better father-son relationship that we can use as an example than the relationship between David and Absalom. As we all know, David was a king. He had gifts as a harpist, but he was not a very good father in that he never disciplined his kids. He made some mistakes that he later regretted, but it was too late. He was just not a very sensitive father. He had an affair with Bathsheba (2 Samuel 11); he sent her husband, Uriah, to battle so that he would be killed. This sin problem began to haunt David in very disturbing ways. In 2 Samuel 13, we read about how his daughter Tamar was raped by her brother Amnon. After hearing about the rape, the other brother, Absalom, was angry with his father for never doing anything about it. Two years later, Absalom had his men kill Amnon, and then he fled to Geshur and then to Jerusalem. For five years he didn't see his father.

No letters, no rides in the chariot, no conversations, no nothing; no wonder Absalom grew up with issues. In 2 Samuel 13: 38–39, we read that Absalom ran to Geshur. Perhaps what he was doing was not running from his father but running to his father. Maybe he thought his father would seek him out. Many of our young men are doing something like that today. Maybe they get in trouble on purpose to compel their fathers to go to them. Maybe they act up in school on purpose and get failing grades to attract their fathers' attention. When a man spends time with his children, it changes their behavior and increases their self-esteem.

A study conducted by a Christian newspaper involved 105 mothers, fathers, and their children over age fourteen. It found that a father's self-esteem is more critical than a mother's in the way children feel about themselves. Children who walk around with their heads down and with no social skills are usually without fathers, so we need fathers.

In verse 39, King David longed to go to Absalom, but it never says he did. He was over Amnon's death, but he was still in an internal battle. Was he supposed to practice a parent's affection or royal duty? That was the pivotal question for him. It was no time to worry about what people would think. His son has left and was in exile because he was afraid of what the people were saying and what his father might say.

So was David supposed to practice parental affection or royal duty? Was he supposed to pardon his son and deal with public opinion, or punish him as a king should have done? This was no time for David to be the king; he was supposed to be a father; that was his time to be a daddy. When we go home, parents, we should leave our work responsibilities at the office. When our children need us, they need us, and that's more important than our work, whatever it is. As far as I'm concerned, my children don't want a pastor at home, they don't want to come home and always feel like they are at church; they want a daddy. Absalom needed a father, not a king. The king was for others; his daddy was for him.

Absalom left Geshur after three years and went to Jerusalem for two. That's five years David didn't see his son, and two days is too long. David had forgotten the color of his son's eyes and hair and what his smile looked like. He had missed watching his son grow up. I want fathers to know today that we have missed watching our sons grow up long enough. Now's the time to show up, and show up with interest. That means paying child support with interest, medical bills with interest, tuition with interest, and graduation costs with interest. We should show up with interest and get interested all over.

I have good news for those of us whose fathers were not there for them. You do have a Father; his name is God. The Bible says in Psalm 27:10, "When my Mother and Father forsake me the Lord will take me up."

Chapter 17

Deadbeat to Upbeat

Luke 15:20–28

In her book *It Takes a Church to Raise a Village*, Dr. Marva Mitchell called the community around us the village. She wrote because she was trying to move the church into the mission field of the village, and to do that, she made several profound points, including that the church must stop having church and start being the church. She wrote that there were gangs in the village that destroyed the lives of her youth with drive-by shootings while the church just drove by, oblivious to those lying wasted in the streets.

Mitchell wrote that the reason we can't curtail this is because we are more concerned about the village breaking into our beautiful facilities than about breaking out into the neighborhood with the power of the glorious gospel of our Lord. She wrote that her book was not intended to be a put-down of the church but a get-up for the church that would halt and reverse the decay of the village.

We spend a lot of time talking about deadbeat dads when we really should be speaking about deadbeat churches. If churches aren't doing anything for the community and our young people, they are nothing more than deadbeat churches, but if we empower our churches, they then can empower fathers and men. Our churches, however, can become empowered only by the Holy Spirit.

The Holy Spirit comes to bring power to individuals who make up the church, not the church building, and if we don't have that power, we're walking around looking physically holy but are spiritually dead.

This Scripture is a classic. Parables, of course, are fabrications told by Jesus to hide the truth from some and to reveal the truth to others, and in this chapter, he offered three parables—the lost sheep, the lost coin, and the lost son. All three had the same theme: God's love for the outcast, the sinners, and they all used the same key words: *lost*, *found*, *rejoice*, and *celebrate*.

I want to focus on the lost son. He wanted his portion of the inheritance early. That meant he would receive a third of his father's inheritance and the older would receive two thirds. Deuteronomy 21 talks a little more about that. For this to happen, it meant that the father had to sell some of his land for cash. This younger son got his money and wasted it in a matter of days.

What I see in the text is a deadbeat son and an upbeat father. This younger son didn't work like his older brother did. He always had his mind on what he could get and what was his. He obviously liked to party, and he spent money that he hadn't earned. Deadbeats like to spend other folks' money, and many deadbeats are womanizers. This deadbeat son spent his money on prostitutes.

But the father was upbeat; he had worked for what he had. He raised his two sons seemingly by himself. He was a hard worker and loved both his sons. When the younger son finally came to his senses, he realized he had broken the fifth commandment, honor thy father and mother.

Read verse 20. His father saw him when he was coming home. Even though the father had given him his share, maybe the father had given him not enough, and the son had run out of funds. Sometimes, the Lord will give us enough to run out. He gives us more than enough and will open up the window of heaven, but we have to earn that. This son had not earned his inheritance, and the father knew his son was going to come back home. He knew like a good father that his money was going to last only so long. He knew that his son would need him before he needed his son.

I can imagine the father checking the front yard, checking his watch, looking out the window, staying up late each night, wondering if it would be the night his son would come home because he had given him enough to run out. Every now and then, God does that. He gives us what we ask for even though we aren't ready to handle it just to compel us back to him, because when we run out, we must run back to God.

When the son came home in verse 22, he has a statement all prepared for his father about how he had messed up, but the father was so excited to see him that he ran to his son. He didn't let his son get his speech out before he kissed him. The father treated the son as if he had been gone for years when he had been gone only for days.

Here's the paradox—the father gave him the best in spite of the son's bad behavior. That's the opposite of man; we give the best for good behavior, but God gives the best for bad behavior. The son got a robe for honor, a ring for power, and sandals to set him apart from the barefoot servants. I don't understand it. He messed up and still was blessed. Well, don't get mad about it; we do the same thing—we mess up and still get blessed. In fact, it wasn't too many days ago that we messed up last, but the Lord didn't withdraw his hand from us. Instead, he extended his wonderful grace to us.

When the son came back, nobody asked where he had been or talked about how he had not been there lately. Sometimes, we make people who haven't been to church lately feel guilty about not having been there, but they will feel guilty on their own. The father said that this son of his had been dead but then was alive again. The son had moved from deadbeat to upbeat, and that called for a celebration in the father's mind.

I want to say to all today that church is not church without a celebration. Every time somebody joins the church, we should celebrate, and every time somebody who has been gone comes back, we ought to celebrate. That's what the angels do whenever one sinner repents (Luke 15:10). I like what this father does; he taught us how to celebrate the accomplishments of ours even when they've done wrong.

The official flower for Father's Day is a dandelion, because the more they are trampled upon, the better they grow.

Chapter 18

Like Father, Like Son

Psalm 72:1

In 1 Samuel 16:11, we read a familiar story about a father who had eight sons. The father's name was Jesse, and it was time for Samuel the priest to anoint a new king. He was told by the Lord to stop mourning; Saul was to fill his horn up with oil and go to Jesse's house, where he would find the next king. Saul wasn't supposed to consider his outward appearance; man looks at the outside, but God looks at the inside.

So Jesse had seven of his eight sons pass before Samuel. One after another, the Lord said to Samuel, "He is not the one." Finally, Samuel asked Jesse, "Do you have any more sons?" He said, "Yes, my youngest boy, but he's taking care of the sheep." David was brought in, and even though he was the youngest and the frailest, he was anointed king.

Here's what I want you to see in that story. Jesse never even considered his son David as the next king. He left David to take care of the sheep and made the assumption that David was too skinny and young to be the next king. Samuel, however, saw more good qualities in David than Jesse did.

What do children do when they are ignored by their fathers? Surely, David could have grown up with psychological imbalances. He could have grown up hating his father; after all, his father never considered him kingly material. If we were to do an analysis of many of our troubled youth today, I guarantee you that we'd find the reason so many of our young people today are in trouble, in gangs, and on drugs is because they are trying to fill the void of not having fathers in their lives. But David overcame the odds, for his heavenly Father discovered in him qualities that his earthly father had missed.

Don't ignore your Father's Day. Maybe Jesse was dealing with his issues back then, but we must get past our issues, for the Lord has called us to love our fathers. It is so much better to make up than to break up.

David then did something his own father possibly didn't do for him. He prayed for his son. This psalm is all about a prayer of a father for his child, and it was this father's dying request or blessing upon Solomon. His son was a bequest. It was common for patriarchs in the Old Testament to leave their children bequests, but that was not an issue for David here. He was already a king, and his son Solomon was already the heir to his dynasty; that's why he was called the royal son here. This prayer for his son was not one for the dynasty but one for the divinity.

David understood that there were some things the dynasty couldn't get you through. The dynasty can't get you through financial disaster; it can't get you through divorces; it can't get you through social challenges. Dynasty can't get you through satanic harassment and evil influences, but the Spirit can.

So in his prayer, he made no reference to the dynasty, but it was replete with spiritual overtures to justice and righteousness. He prayed for justice for himself but righteousness for his son, and in the process, he taught his son about prayer. The best inheritance a father can give his children is the concept of a prayer life. Not a house, not a new car or money, not new clothes, not a fishing trip or a shopping spree—fathers need to teach their children how to pray.

Don't misunderstand me—there's nothing wrong with giving our children things, but if we give them too much too soon, we can lead them to believe they can get whatever they want without working for it, and that's dangerous, because then, we're teaching our children the "give me" concept—give me this and give me that.

A little boy was always asking God for things when he prayed; he would say, "God, give me this and give me that." His mother told him, "Son, don't ask God for so many things. Just report for duty."

When we teach our children how to pray, we are teaching them how to report for duty. And when they report for duty, the Lord will reward them according to their labor. God is looking for some people who will show up for duty, and when they show up, they have to be dressed accordingly. Their feet must be shod with the preparation of the gospel of peace. They have to be wearing their helmet of salvation and holding the sword of the Spirit, which is the Word of God. They must be wearing the belt of truth and the breastplate of righteousness. If you want the Lord to bless you, show up for duty.

So David was praying this prayer to teach his son how to pray, and notice that David called his son a royal son, for after all, David was the king. That made his son an heir to the royal throne. Well, that kind of sounds like we are the Lord's children. God is King, and we are his children; we have been adopted into the royal family. We will then be treated like royalty, and God is looking for fathers who will treat their children like royalty. That means when we raise our children like royalty, they will expect certain things and not settle for anything less.

Let's teach our children not to settle for lives of poverty, minimum-wage jobs, just high school diplomas, lazy and no-good men or women, or backseats anywhere. We are royalty, and our King can supply our every need.

As David prepared for his son to become his successor, he understood that his own righteousness was not good enough for his son, and that is why he prayed that his son would be endowed with the Lord's righteousness. For like the prophet Isaiah said in Isaiah 64:6, we are all like unclean things and all our righteousness is like filthy rags. He understood like Paul said in Romans 3:10 that there was no one righteousness—no one. He realized that if Solomon remained on his own, he was going to mess up, but if he turned him over to the Lord, some of the Lord's influence would rub off on him.

Let me say a word to the parents today—stop stressing over your children. Turn them over to Jesus, for the Bible is true, and Proverbs 22:6 says we should train up our children in the way they should go, and when they are old, they will not depart from it.

All we can do is train them up and let them go. We can have faith that one day they will come home. Look at the Prodigal Son. Regardless of what he had done, he came back home, and his daddy was waiting on him. God is looking for some daddies who will stand in the front yard and look for their children to come home. These fathers will say, "I don't care what you did. Come on in to your father's house, where you will find love, peace, and joy forever."

Chapter 19

Rich Dad, Poor Dad

Proverbs 13:7–8

In *Rich Dad Poor Dad*, Robert Kiyosaki wrote about financial independence by means of investing and real estate. After watching his father go from a PhD and head of his academic department to dying with nothing, he learned about money from his father's friend, someone who hadn't finished eighth grade. He became the rich dad while his father was the poor dad.

I'm sure every father can concur with me that money doesn't make us happy; it's watching our children grow up well that makes us happy. That can happen only when we as fathers have grown in the Lord.

One problem with fathers is that too many are so busy providing for their children that they neglect out of naïveté the most important part of being a father—the nurturing aspect. I know that God has made women to be nurturers. That gift was given to them by God, but men must also learn how to become nurturers, and the best example for teaching fatherhood and the nurturing aspect of fatherhood is the penguin.

After emperor penguins mate, the female lays one egg, which she gives to the father very carefully so the egg doesn't break. She leaves to eat. The egg sits on top of the fathers' feet and under his brood flap. The father emperor penguin incubates the egg in the middle of freezing weather, and he does this by standing in a tight huddle for two to three months straight.

During this time, the fathers don't eat anything; they take just a little snow for moisture. When the chicks finally hatch, they are hungry. The father then regurgitates a white secretion and feeds it to the chicks. When the mother comes back to get her chick, the father carefully turns the chick over to its mother, not letting the chick hit the snow and ice, which would kill it. Once the mother has the chick, the father leaves to get some food. What a tremendous sacrifice of nurture. Can you imagine going months without food? That is not only an example of fatherhood but is also an example of a rich dad.

Rich dads make sacrifices for their children. Psychologist Dr. James Dobson says the average father spends thirty-seven seconds a day with his children while he spends hours watching TV.

We need rich fathers today who will give their children hours and hours, not just seconds. In this text, Solomon was admonishing us and cautioning us on how we should live, and he informed us that too many of us emphasize possessions and wealth to the point that we become pretentious. Notice that both men are pretentious. One pretends to be rich but has nothing, and the other pretends to be poor but is wealthy. This can cause a false sense of security. The rich have some protection for their money, and the poor have little need for protection since they have nothing worth stealing.

This brief text reminds us of Solomon's relationship with his father; David had riches but didn't have a good relationship with his children. David was a good musician, a good warrior, and a great political strategist, but he was not a good father. One of his sons wanted to kill him, his daughter was abused because of his sin, and he lost a son because of an affair. He wanted to build a temple but could not, so the Lord allowed his son Solomon to do it.

Perhaps when Solomon wrote this text, he had his father on his mind. Maybe he was saying we shouldn't be like his father, who had wealth but didn't have his children. We need fathers who are more concerned about their children than their riches. We don't need selfish dads. When we are trying to build up our companies but can't build up our families, when we are trying to make financial investments but never invest in our children's futures, when office hours become more important that the hours we spend with our children, when the boardroom table becomes more important than the dinner table, we fail at being fathers. Solomon was speaking from experience when he wrote this; he was telling the fathers of today not to be like his father, who pretended to be rich when he didn't even have the respect of his children. If we don't have that, we don't have anything.

He wrote about the man who pretended to be poor but was actually wealthy. Any man or father today who has Jesus never has to pretend to be poor. He will never be poor, for when he has Jesus, he will have everything he needs. In 2 Corinthians 8:9, we read this point clearly; though Jesus was rich, for our sake, he became poor so that through his poverty we would become rich. Jesus transferred his wealth to us—a direct-deposit blessing.

I know fathers, mothers, and grandparents who are rich by direct deposit, the Lord. Simply because of who they are, Jesus gives them his wealth. They didn't earn it, they didn't have to give him a blank check, and they didn't have to redeem their points. Jesus doesn't need our bank account numbers; all we have to do is to open our hearts for his deposit.

We need fathers who will open their hearts to God, who will stop making Sundays their day off and start opening their hearts to God. Father who will stop sleeping in on Sundays and allow the Lord to deposit some of his wealth in them. When he does, they can deposit that wealth in the hearts of their children, and they will deposit it into their children. But it all starts with us as men and fathers. That's why Proverbs 13:22 says a good man leaves an inheritance for his children.

It is clear from this verse that we cannot be who we are not; these men were faking it. Galatians 6:3 says that he who thinks he is something when he is nothing deceives himself. When we do that, we become fathers who get convicted but have no conviction. When there is no conviction, we lie, bribe, and politic our way out of stuff. We need fathers of conviction. If we know the baby is ours, then we should take care of it, pay child support, buy diapers, and buy some milk.

An old African proverb says that when we follow in the steps of our fathers, we will start to walk like them. We have to live holy, and we have to live righteously, because there are some boys who want to be just like us, and they need spiritually rich fathers to follow.

Chapter 20

A Doting Father's Proclamation

Luke 1:76

Lewis Carroll, an ordained Anglican minister, taught math at Oxford during the day and wrote children's books and fairy tales such as Alice in Wonderland and Humpty Dumpty at night. When I learned that the person who wrote Humpty Dumpty was a minister, I decided to look for the theological interpretations in these childlike stories. Charles Carroll described Humpty Dumpty as an anthropomorphized egg who was depicting a clumsy person. He wrote, "Humpty Dumpty sat on a wall, Humpty Dumpty had great fall. All of the king's horses and all of the king's men couldn't put Humpty back together again." Here is my issue—they called the king's horses and men, but nobody called the king.

Some jobs only a king can handle. Too often, we call the king as a last resort rather than as our first choice. When we lose our jobs, we file for unemployment before we believe God to be our Jehovah Jireh, our provider. When we get hungry, we get food stamps before we ask him to do for us what he did with the five loaves and two fishes. He fed the multitude and still had baskets left over because he knew how to turn a little into a lot.

These verses before us are known in Latin as the Benedictus, "invocation" and "blessing." It's a song being sung by Zechariah, and it is filled with Old Testament quotations and allusions. In it, Zechariah, the father of John the Baptist, described the deliverance of God's people through the Messiah. The father was introducing his son to the world just as his son would introduce Jesus to the world. The Messiah he described was to be according to verse 68 a horn of salvation. The horns of an animal symbolized its power, so the Messiah would be strong and would deliver the nation from its enemies.

After receiving the news from the angel Gabriel that his wife was going to conceive in her old age and how great his son was going to be, Zechariah did not believe it. According to Luke 1:20, it cost him his speech for a while. The angel took away his voice until John's calling was fulfilled. The angel took away his voice because even though he had prayed for a son, he didn't want to accept his son's mission. Gabriel told him, "You will be silent and unable to speak until the day this happens."

Too many of us men have lost our voices. We have been silent for too long, silent about child support, silent about spending quality time with our children, and silent in church. We see more women in most churches than we see men. We have lost our voice. Dr. Michelle Alexander, a professor at Ohio State and legal scholar, wrote *The New Jim Crow*. In her book, she wrote that there were more African-American men in prison or involved in the legal system than were enslaved in 1850. No wonder the sisters can't find a decent man—they're all in prison. It's time though for men to get their voices back. I'm glad today that some men set the precedent that it pays to serve the Lord.

So Zechariah got his voice back. He believed then the proclamation from Gabriel, and in these verses, he was a proud father because he understood what his son John the Baptist was to do. He said in verse 76, "You my child will be called a prophet."

Now this is what I see—a father speaking destiny into his son's life. We are called to speak destiny into our children likewise. If at age twenty or so, they don't know what they want to be, we must speak it into them, "You'll be someone great. You will be an attorney, a police officer, a judge, a physician, or an educator." We must help them decide where they want to go to college. "I see Morehouse in your future," or "I see Spellman in your future," or "I see Paul Quinn College or another black college, or Harvard or Yale in your future."

Proverbs 18:21 says death and life are in the power of the tongue. That's what God did when it came to his Son Jesus, for in Isaiah 9:6, he spoke destiny into his life and said, "You shall be called Wonderful, Mighty God, Prince of Peace the Everlasting Father!"

In that same verse, we learn that John the Baptist was to prepare the way for Jesus. In biblical days, when a king was coming to a place, he would send a herald ahead to announce his arrival. The herald's job was to announce and to prepare. He would shout, "The king is coming!" while he cleared the streets of stones and stumbling blocks. That was what John was doing—preparing us for Jesus.

It's like praise and worship—we need both. *Praise* means "to adore" and "to approve"; *worship* is how we express our love for God. Praise is the way to worship, and worship is the way to an encounter with the living God. *Proskuneo* is the Greek word for "to worship"; it means to lay prostrate before the Lord or to kiss the hand. It's a sign of affection.

Here's the point: to prepare for Jesus, we must prostrate, not procrastinate. Too many of us have missed blessings because of our procrastination, and many people will be in hell because of procrastination. I learned a long time ago that procrastination is the thief of time, but worse, it's also the thief of souls. We must lie before him and worship.

There is no time like the present to worship the Lord. We can't change what happened yesterday, but we can take charge of what we will do tomorrow. Hebrews 3:15 says that on the day we hear his voice, we should be sure not to harden our hearts. Today, while blood is running warm in our veins, today, while we still have a chance for the greatest miracle that the Lord has given us, we should wait on him.

Sarah was eight when Joshua was two. They lived in the country by a lake. The father went in the house and told his children to stay away from the water. Shortly thereafter, Joshua ran in the house. He couldn't talk much; he just said, "Sarah—water." The father ran outside, jumped in the water, swam to the bottom, pulled his little girl's fingers away from an old wheel axle, brought her back on land, gave her mouth-to-mouth, and asked, "What were you doing there all that time?" She said, "Waiting for you, Daddy, waiting for you."

The king is coming. I don't know when he will arrive, but let's just all wait on him.

Chapter 21

Come and Go with Me to My Father's House

John 1:40–42

All of us should be familiar with the story in John 4, about the Samaritan woman who had an encounter with Jesus at the well. He asked her for a drink, and she said, "I am a Samaritan and you are a Jew. How can you ask me for a drink?" He said, "If you knew the gift of God and knew who it was asking you for a drink, you would have asked and I would have given you living water." The woman said, "Sir you have nothing to draw the water from the well with. Are you greater than Jacob who gave us this well and drank from it himself?" Jesus said, "Whoever drinks from this well shall thirst again, but whoever drinks from the water that I shall give shall never thirst again."

That sounded good to the woman. She said, "Give me this water so that I do not have to keep coming here drawing water." Jesus said, "Now go tell your husband this good news." She said, "I don't have a husband." Jesus said, "Right. As a matter of fact, you've been married five times, and the one you are with now is not your husband." She left her water jar, went back to her town, and said to the people, "Come see a man who told me everything I ever did."

Can you imagine how the people were looking at her? She had been married five times and was considered an outcast by some, but she was sharing Jesus with the whole town. Anybody can talk about Jesus; no one needs a long résumé to talk about him. All anyone needs is an encounter with him. Your background is not important, just an encounter, and when you have had an encounter with Jesus, you will want everybody to know about the man who changed you from a nobody to a somebody, a nothing to a something, a sinner to a winner, from a scar to a star. Everybody needs to know about Jesus.

All this woman did was invite others to meet a friend who had changed her life. When was the last time you invited someone to meet Jesus? When was the last time you invited someone to church, Bible study, prayer meeting, or Sunday school? Remember, to invite somebody into a group means you first must be a part of that group.

Our text today is Andrew, one of the twelve disciples. Not much is known about him. No book in the Bible is named after him, no monument was built in his honor, he was not talked about a lot in Scripture, but he is known for one thing—he was always bringing someone to Jesus. This is why Jesus told his disciples, "Follow me and I will make you fishers of men."

When we bring others to Christ, we become fishers of men. Andrew was a fisherman who didn't stop fishing; he just changed bait. God doesn't have to change our professions to make us effective; he will use us in whatever area we are in. Andrew started out as a disciple of John the Baptist, but after John the Baptist told him about Jesus being the Lamb of God, Andrew started following Jesus, and when he learned more about Jesus, he felt positively compelled to spread the news. I'd like to think that whenever Andrew was talking about Jesus, he was saying, "Come with me to my father's house."

Jesus was so important to Andrew that before he told anybody about Jesus, he told his brother Simon (verse 41). When we talk about Jesus and invite others to our father's house, we need to begin with our own households, our own families. It's time for us to start saving our own households. Andrew found his brother first, and we need to follow suit.

I know it can be difficult to convert our families. Sometimes, those we are closest to are the most difficult to save. Sometimes, our greatest opposition will come from those we love; that's why Matthew 10:36 says that a man's enemies will be of his own household.

Jesus learned that when he went home and discovered that prophets were without honor in their hometowns and in their houses. According to Matthew 13:57, our families know us better than anybody else does. They've watched us grow up. They will tell us, "I dare you witness to me about the Lord."

Andrew probably had to contend with all that, but in spite of it, he witnessed to his brother. We all have family members who need to be saved. Let's start talking about Jesus to the family first and invite the family to church. What if they don't want to go? Then we should just keep being good examples of Christians, and by our fruits they will be persuaded.

When he found his brother and declared who Jesus was, he was making a statement that he was not ashamed of the gospel or of Christ. Don't be ashamed of Christ. It is a huge mistake to be ashamed of Christ, for if we are ashamed of him, he will be ashamed of us. Oh how embarrassing it would be to hear him say on judgment day, "Get away from me. I never knew you." To be ashamed of him is to hide him, and Luke 11:33 says that no one lights a lamp and puts it in a place where it will be hidden. Instead, he puts it on its stand so that those who come in may see the light. Don't hide him. Every time we refrain from talking about Jesus, we are hiding him. When we refuse to testify of him, we are hiding him. When we try to keep him to ourselves, we are hiding him. When the world does not know that we are Christians by our love, we are hiding him. When our coworkers don't know we are Christians or what church we go to, we are hiding him.

It's time to bring Jesus out of the dark, where he has been too long. It's time to move him to the front of the line; he's been at the back long enough. It's time to talk about him. We've been silent too long, but the Bible says let the redeemed of the Lord say so.

I like Andrew's aggression. He was so aggressive that he didn't wait for his brother to come to him; rather, he went to his brother. We need to follow that example and learn how to take the gospel to the masses, to the streets, to the lost. We cannot wait for them to come to the gospel on their own.

Andrew fulfilled Scripture when Jesus said that if he was lifted up from the earth, that would draw all men to him. Every time we talk about Jesus, we are lifting him up—we are reminding the world of his crucifixion, death, and resurrection. So let us all lift him up.

Chapter 22

My Hair Got in the Way

2 Samuel 14:25–26, 18:9–15

In 2 Samuel 14:25–26, we read of the macabre vanity of Absalom. He had very long hair. It was so long that five pounds of hair were trimmed from his head annually. He loved his hair. He felt it made him handsome, and he was handsome, a fine physical specimen. He was so into himself that he didn't care about anybody else. Perhaps when Solomon wrote in Ecclesiastes, "Vanity, Vanity. All is vanity," he was speaking of Absalom. Perhaps when Paul wrote in Romans that we were not to think more highly of ourselves than we ought, he was thinking of Absalom. When we start focusing too much of our attention on ourselves, we don't have time for anybody else, and no man is an island; no man stands alone. Hezekiah Walker says you need me and I need you.

Absalom didn't have anybody on his mind but himself. All he wanted to do was to take over his father's kingdom and be king. I guess the real tragedy was that he loved his hair more than he loved his father. It's all right to love yourself, but don't get obsessed with yourself.

The text finds Absalom returning from the forest after his men had just been defeated by his father. Twenty thousand men died in the forest that day. David had forewarned his men to be gentle with his son Absalom. Even though his son had tried to take over his kingdom, even though his son had tried to defeat his father in battle, even though

Absalom had formed a conspiracy against his father, David still told his men that if they got to him before he did, they were to be gentle with him, for he was still David's son (verse 5). David knew Absalom deserved death; that was what justice demanded, but he didn't want him dead.

It's like the mother who went to court to plead for her son, who was on trial for a terrible crime. The mother begged the judge not to give her son the death penalty. The judge said, "Ma'am, I sympathize with you, but justice demands that your son die." She said, "I'm not asking for justice. I'm asking for mercy." This is what David was saying in verse 5—show my son some mercy.

If we are honest with ourselves, we will admit we've been in the same predicament. All of us have messed up, made some major mistakes, and committed some terrible sins, but our God showed us mercy and grace and sent his Son into the world that we might have one more chance.

Absalom, knowing that his men had been defeated, noticed he was surrounded by his father's men. He learned a lesson he would take to his grave: the father always wins. The father is more experienced, has more patience, has more political connections, and has more discipline. He cannot be outmaneuvered or outrun. The father thinks better and executes better because he is wiser and stronger.

Some sons think, as Absalom did, that they can defeat their fathers. They might win a battle but never the whole war. Daddy always wins, and that's why the Prodigal Son in Luke 15 had to go home to his father after failing to make it in the world on his own. He got caught up with the wrong crowd and spent his money on the wrong things. He ran out of food and friends. But Scripture says that when he came to himself, he went home to his father, who had been waiting for him to come home.

Every child who has a home needs to give God praise that he or she has a home. All children who have homes—places to lay their heads, places to eat—need to put their hands together and give God praise for what they have.

So Absalom jabbed his spurs into the mule's sides in verse 9, making him take off. But he didn't realize that his mule was carrying him to his own destruction. His head—his thick hair—got entangled in some tree branches. His thick hair, his source of pride, led him to his demise.

Whatever we are caught up in is the thing that will kill us. Absalom was into his hair. He was jealous, ambitious, vain, and power hungry, and all that led him to his death. What are you caught up in? Politics? Money? Gambling? Drugs? Be careful, because those things can lead to your destruction.

Perhaps God got tired of sharing his time with Absalom's hair. Perhaps Absalom spent more time with his hair than he did in getting closer to God. Listen—many of us have not been fair to God. We give our hobbies more time than we give God. Golf comes before church, or maybe it's baseball or football that comes before church. Some folks will miss church on Sunday to cheer their favorite team. My response to that is the next time they can't meet the mortgage; they should call their favorite teams. The next time somebody gets sick in their families, they should call their favorite sports heroes. What we are caught up in will lead to our own demise.

Absalom was left hanging in midair as his mule rode into the sunset. Absalom was so mean that his mule told him good riddance. You can't make everybody your friend because some people will leave you hanging. They will say they love you, but when it's time to get married, they'll leave you hanging. They will promise you the rose garden, but all you'll end up with is the thorns. They will be a witness to a crime against you, but when it's time to testify on your behalf, they will leave you hanging. But while you're hanging, just hang in there. That's because the one who said, "I'll never leave you or forsake you" will come to your rescue.

Absalom was left hanging between earth and heaven because neither wanted anything to do with him. His mule had left him, earth would not keep him, heaven would not take him, so hell received him. As he was hanging, he was unable to defend himself, and he was killed by Joab and his armor bearers, who plunged three javelins into his heart. Absalom died all alone, and evil will eventually leave you all by yourself. He died and probably went to hell because his ego and his hair had gotten in the way.

I want to make sure all children of God know they don't have to worry about anything getting in their way. All they have to do is read Matthew 17:20. If we have the faith the size of a mustard seed, we can say to the mountain, "Move!"

Chapter 23

Man on the Run

2 Samuel 15:13–14

When we hear or read about a person who's on the run, we think about a fugitive running from the law. Back in the 1960s, there was a TV series, *The Fugitive*, and in recent years, there was a movie with the same theme. It was about a man by the name of Dr. Kimble, who had been falsely accused of killing his wife. He finds himself running from the police and trying to find the real culprit, a one-armed man, who was getting away. The movie takes us through the perils of deception and false accusations. Sometimes, we all find ourselves running from things we didn't do. Those things have a way of coming back to embarrass and haunt us, such as David not being there for his son. Sometimes, if we aren't careful, what we're running from will run us.

This is where we find ourselves in this text from 2 Samuel. Absalom's conspiracy to take over his father's throne had gained momentum. He had successfully won the people over in the early verses of this chapter, and he led an invasion against Jerusalem that forced David to flee for his life because David had been too busy with his royal responsibilities to discipline his son. That is the thesis of this father-and-son saga.

David had never disciplined any of his sons. He hadn't disciplined Amnon for raping his sister, and he never disciplined Absalom for causing his men to kill Amnon. Lack of discipline will always cause a revolt in the family, because a family with no discipline is a family without leadership. David was a good king, a good man of valor, but he was a terrible father, and he was paying for his sins through the dysfunction of Absalom. His son Amon had raped his own sister (2 Samuel 13) because of David's sin with Bathsheba (2 Samuel 11).

Where there is no leadership in the family, we have a confused family that doesn't know who is in charge, and that's exactly what we read about in this text. David had control of his kingdom, but he had lost control of his family. So Absalom was acting like the father, while David was acting like the son.

Isn't that the way it is in many of our homes today? Nobody knows who's in charge anymore. Daughters are mouthing off to their mothers, and sons are mouthing off to their fathers. I don't understand this era. The way some children talk to their parents is ridiculous; they show no respect to their parents. When I was coming up, all my father or mother had to do when we were acting up in church was just look at us. But nowadays, the children look at the parents, and the parents get scared!

Lack of discipline causes parents to be submissive to children, and that's what happened with Absalom and David in this text. Look at verse 14, when David heard that the people were with Absalom. He said, "Come, we must flee." Hear me today. A real father does not run from his son; a real father leads his son. He does so by precept, by example. He leads his son in the way of the cross. He leads his son in prayer. When a father runs from his son, as David did here, he is teaching his son how to become a bully, and the boy grows up thinking that everyone will be afraid of him. That's because when a boy makes his father run from him, he starts thinking he can make anybody run from him. When such a boy gets married, his wife is afraid of him, and his children become afraid of him, and everybody at work gets afraid of him because his father had created a bully.

Hear me when I say we don't need any more bullies. We need fathers who will follow Christ, and we need sons who will follow their fathers as their fathers follow Christ.

Verse 14 has enough information in it for a whole sermon. When David said to his officials, "Come, we must flee," we must understand he was speaking to all his officials and servants. According to verse 18, he was speaking to all his staff and about 600 Gittites, who were from Gath, a Philistine country. They were men of great stature; they were David's bodyguards.

So David had all these people on his side, but when he told them they all had to flee, he made cowards out of them just like he was. That's because people take on their leaders' personalities; one coward turns into many cowards. When David told them they had to flee, he was sending them the wrong message. If he had stayed and fought, so would they have done, but they did what he told them to do. He ran, and so did they.

Listen. We don't need any more cowards. In fact, there should be no cowards in the kingdom. According to 2 Timothy 1:7, God has given us not the spirit of fear but the spirit of power, love, and sound minds.

When David ran, he did so for the wrong reason. You see, when we run, we should never run for cover, because we are already covered. When we run, we should run to get help. We know according to Psalm 46 that God is our refuge and our strength and a very present help in times of any trouble. When we run to God, to church, to the throne of grace, we run to our prayer partners.

The Bible declares in Psalm 110 that God will make our enemies our footstools, so when our enemies get on our backs, they don't realize it, but they are helping us without even knowing it. With every lie they tell, every trap they set, every jealous move they make, they are causing us to move closer to God for the purpose of becoming our footstools. And that will help us step up.

Chapter 24

Move Over, Daddy

2 Samuel 14:32–33, 15:1–5

An African proverb says that if you follow the steps of your father, you will learn to walk like him. We need more sons who will follow the steps of their fathers, but before we do that, we need to make sure the fathers are making the right steps, for what that African proverb means is that our sons will become the same persons we are, and that as fathers, we are the first examples and role models our sons will see. If we talk to our wives in a negative way, they will do the same when they grow up. If we cheat on our wives, they will cheat on theirs. If we abuse our wives, they will abuse theirs. They will think these behaviors are the norm.

We must make the right footsteps for them; we must live our lives with our children in mind. David, who was not a good father, had a tumultuous relationship with Absalom. David was not a disciplinarian; he had had an affair with another man's wife, and as a result, his daughter was raped by her brother, who was killed by his brother Absalom.

To make matters worse, David received a prophecy from Nathan that predicted disaster. In 2 Samuel 12:11, David was told, "Out of your own household I am going to bring calamity upon you. Before your very eyes I will take your wives and give them to one who is close to you and he will lie with your wives in broad daylight." We find this prophecy fulfilled in 2 Samuel 16:21–22, when Absalom slept with his father's royal concubines on the roof of the palace. The baby Bathsheba was pregnant with died.

It appears that David's mistakes and misfortunes were resurfacing in the life of his son. In this chapter, we read about the steps Absalom took to take his father's throne. We discover that Absalom was still angry that his father had not sought him out during his five years away from home after he killed his brother. Absalom was so angry that he delivered an ultimatum to his father in 14:32: accept me or kill me. Absalom was brought to David, who kissed him in verse 33. Absalom was reconciled to the family. But Absalom wanted more; he wanted his father's throne.

I speak to fathers when I say that we have messed up with our children. It's going to take more than a kiss on the head to make everything right. It's going to take more than a kiss to make up for all the times we weren't there. It's going to take more than a kiss to make up for all the ball games and recitals and graduations we missed. A kiss cannot be compared to the quality time we could have spent with our kids. It cannot be compared to tucking them in at night, reading them stories, and teaching them all we can. Don't misunderstand me; there's nothing wrong with affection, but when you have not had it in so long, it becomes reverse abuse. What most children would love another child may detest.

In this text, Absalom was angry because his father had not been there for him, so he conspires to take his father's throne. Notice how he did it in 15:1; he provided himself with chariots, horses, and fifty men to run before him. Let us look at this verse with a psychological rather than a theological eye. Absalom was already angry with his father because he had never been there for him. David considered his kingdom more important than his family. David had never disciplined Absalom, and after five years, David was slow in building a relationship with Absalom, so Absalom used the thing he despised in his father to get his father's throne.

Beware of the king's kid syndrome. That's when the child hates what we do because what we do takes us from them, so they pretend to like what we do when the whole time they are using what they hate to destroy us. Yes, hate. He despised the king in his father, so he acted like a king so in due time he could tell his father, "Move over, Daddy."

Absalom did not want to be a king because his father was a king; he wanted to be a king to satisfy his own ambition. Some children want to be just like their fathers, but they have the wrong motives.

In verse 6, Absalom tried to overthrow his father by stealing the hearts of the people. He tried to placate the people; he kissed them and acted as if he cared for them and wanted them to bring their complaints to him for royal adjudication. Absalom knew that if he could steal the hearts of the people, they would turn against his father.

And of course the people started eating out of Absalom's hand. To make matters worse, after doing all of that for four years, he decided it was time to take his father's throne. He asked his father's permission to go to Hebron, where David had been anointed. The place where David had been anointed became the place where Absalom took over the throne.

Don't worry about these kinds of situations; keep in mind that Romans 8:31 is true: if God is for us, who can be against us?

Chapter 25

The Danger of Unresolved Grief

2 Samuel 19:1–8

As we continue this father-and-son saga of David and his son Absalom, we come to a very serious point at which one party becomes selfish and the other heartless. David was grieving Absalom's death; he had temporarily forgotten about everything else and was being selfish. General Joab's soldiers were heartless; they didn't care a bit about Absalom's death. He was nothing to them, just another casualty of war, and they were unsympathetic to David. Someone once said there was a vast difference between putting your nose in other people's business and putting your heart into other people's problems; we see the truth of that statement, for Joab his men were ruthless, which made them heartless.

We Christians ought never be selfish or heartless and go through life with cavalier attitudes about others' feelings. Everyone deserves to be treated with dignity and respect because we never know when we might find ourselves in need of that ourselves. Our challenge is to live the words of the apostle Paul in Romans 12:15—rejoice with those who rejoice and weep with those who weep.

In our text, we find David mourning his son's death. He had to have known deep in his heart that was going to occur, but that didn't change the fact that Absalom had been his flesh and blood. Perhaps he was weeping because he realized he hadn't done a good job of raising his son or because he figured out his son's problems were a direct result of his own sins and mistakes. Perhaps he was weeping because he wanted to have died in place of his son. David's mourning caused the soldiers who had fought for him and saved his life to lose respect for him and lose their joy they had in winning another war.

If we are not careful, those who are experiencing difficulties will try to bring us into their predicaments just because they are broken themselves. They will make us feel guilty because we have a car and they have to take buses. They will make us feel guilty for having jobs while they're unemployed. Anybody know anybody like that? Sometimes, they will be members of our own families. They're going through hard times, and if we aren't careful, they'll make it our fault because they're looking for someone to blame.

This is where David found himself—weeping and subconsciously trying to pull the soldiers into his grief, but it was not working. In verses 5 and 6, Joab admonished David. David was so into his own problems that he overlooked the people who had risked their lives for him; we ought to be careful not to do that. We should not forget about those who have gone before us, as David had forgotten his soldiers and his general, who had saved his life, and he forgot his family. Max Lucado wrote the book *It's Not about You*. In it, he detailed this concept a little more. When we think it's all about us, we don't care how many people we crush trying to get to the top. We don't care about hurting others' feelings, and we don't care about how many people we lie on, because all that matters is what we're going through. If that's your position, you're living in a fool's paradise. But Hezekiah Walker told me to remind us today of the words in his song "You need me and I need you." We are all a part of God's family.

Joab didn't care about being insubordinate in front of David; he just told the king what was on his mind and told David in essence, "Get up, David. Encourage your men. If you don't, they'll walk out on you." In verse 7, Joab sounded harsh, but all he was really saying to David was, "Get up and stop feeling sorry for yourself. God has been too good to you to cry your eyes out." Our parents may be gone, our brothers and sisters may be gone, but the Lord has left us here and has given us one more day. He may not give us fifteen more years as he gave Hezekiah, or

Moses, who died at age 120, or Sarah, who died at age 127, or Abraham, who died at age 175, but he has given you at least one more day to say, "Just another day the Lord has made."

When David was weeping, did he stop to realize that perhaps God had Joab and his men show up not to help him mourn but to help him get through his mourning? God doesn't send people our way to help us mourn. If he did, that would turn a potential breakthrough into a pity party. You understand—you invite your friends over, I invite my friends over, and we all just mourn together in a great, big pity party. No. When God sends people our way during our hard times, he does so that they can pray us through, fast us through, anoint us with oil through, and lay hands on us so we can make it through. He is not a God of depression, he is a God of possession who wants us to possess the best.

I didn't understand what was occurring in this text until I read more. I thought that this text was merely about David's mourning over his son and that the soldiers were there to help him through his grief. That's partially accurate, but it all becomes clearer when we glance at the next chapter. There was a troublemaker named Sheba, who became David's next battle. His defeat of Absalom prepared him for his next battle. Every victory in life is simply God's way of preparing us for the next battle. It was so important for David to get through his grieving process to end up prepared for his next fight. Whatever we are involved in right now is just our practice run. God is teaching us how to fight right now.

You have to get through your weeping and grieving if you're going to be successful in your next battle. Perhaps the song writer Horatio R. Palmer in his hymn entitled "Yield not to temptation", said it best when he wrote yield not to temptation, for all yielding is sin. Each victory will help you some other to win fight manfully onward dark passions subdue look ever to Jesus he will carry you through."

Chapter 26

I Have Some Bad News

2 Samuel 18:29–33

None of us is immune to bad news. When this nation was attacked by terrorists on that dreadful day, September 11, 2001, that was bad news. On July 7, 2005, in London, the nation listened as terrorists attacked a subway with three bombs; 700 were wounded and 37 killed. These incidents are just two examples of bad news, but unfortunately, some folks are not bothered by bad news unless it happens to them or someone they know directly. There comes a time in everyone's life when he or she must stand between the corridors of possibility and reality and face the fact that one day he or she will be on the receiving end of some bad news.

Bad news. It comes when we least expect it. It comes in the middle of the night, early in the morning, or late in the day when we're sitting down to dinner. It interrupts whatever we're doing. It's no respecter of person, gender, race, creed, or denomination; it just comes. But sometimes, bad news can be used as an opportunity to uncover some profound truths. This was the case of H. S. Spafford, who learned his wife and children had been killed while on a yacht. He asked the Coast Guard to take him to spot on the water where his family had died. He wrote these words from that sentimental place on the water: "When peace like a river attendeth my way, when sorrow like sea billows roll, whatever my lot, thou has taught me to say it is well, it is well with my soul."

God often has a way of using one person's bad news as a means to help and encourage somebody else. In our text, David has just learned of the death of Absalom, whom Joab and his armor bearers had killed with javelins. Absalom was David's third son killed as a result of David's sins with Bathsheba and against her husband, Uriah. His first son, remember, died when Bathsheba became pregnant as a result of their affair, and he was told by Nathan that his son was going to die in 2 Samuel 12. Even though David fasted and prayed that the Lord would not take his son, he did, because when God makes his mind up to do something, not even fasting and prayer can change his mind. His second son, Amnon, was killed by Absalom for raping his own sister (2 Samuel 13). In this text, Absalom was killed by Joab, David's general.

One of Joab's men, Ahimazz, was so elated that Absalom and his men had been killed that he asked Joab three times if he could be the messenger of the news to David. Joab allowed Ahimazz to do so, but Joab also sent a Cushite to report to King David.

Because Ahimazz was an athlete known for his speed, he outran the Cushite and got to David first. The king asked about his son, but Ahimazz didn't tell him his son was dead; he told him there had been great confusion. David learned the news of Absalom from the Cushite. I can only imagine that the Cushite prefaced his words with, "I have some bad news."

We must admire the ethics of this Cushite. Notice that he never disclosed to David how Absalom had been killed. He didn't say, "Let me tell you what happened. He was hanging by his hair from a tree, and Joab stabbed him with a javelin, and the rest of us finished him off." No. The Cushite knew there was a right way to give bad news.

God wants us to be caring, empathic, and sympathetic. Everyone is not called to be a messenger because God cannot entrust his message to everyone, just those who know how to give messages in love. Messengers must know how to rebuke, reproof, and admonish with love. They must understand that the messages they give can be hopeful or destructive; they can be messages of light or messages of darkness. This Cushite was the model messenger.

When David learned his son was dead (verse 33), he was literally shaking because of his loss. He wept in private. He allowed himself to become overwhelmed with the bad news. He allowed it to control his life. We should not allow bad news to make our lives bad; if we do, then we will find ourselves obsessed with bad news. Some people can become obsessed with hearing bad news and want to learn all they can of it. They can't want to hear who was shot, whose marriage is not working, whose child is in jail, who died this week, or who is sick. They actually seek out bad news. People like that scare me; it says to me that they're living their lives with and in bad news and that they have been around so much bad news they don't know how to respond to anything positive.

It's time to share some good news—Jesus saves. That's good news. He forgives no matter what we have done, and that's good news too. He died on the cross for us, and that's more good news. He refused to stay in the tomb, and that's great news. He is a healer, a provider, and our Savior, and that's the best news ever.

David was weeping and thinking about what he should have done when Absalom was young. Listen to what he said: "Absalom my son, my son, if only I had died instead of you oh Absalom my son, my son!" He called him son four times in one verse. He acknowledged him as his son, but it was too late; David had waited too long to do that.

We should not wait until our children are dead before we call them our children. We should not wait until they are in comas on their deathbeds before we tell them how much we love them. We should acknowledge them while they can hear us and see us and feel us. If only Absalom would have heard those words while he was trying to take over his father's kingdom, if only Absalom would have heard those words when he was trying to fight with his father, if only Absalom would have heard those words when he was growing up, perhaps things would have turned out way different.

When David said that he wished he had died instead of Absalom, he was standing in the gap for his son. We need to stand in the gap before it's too late. We should pray for our children even when they are not with us; by doing so, we will be standing in the gap for them. Their problems will become ours, their plights will become ours, and their struggles will become ours. That's what fathers should do—stand in the gap for their children.

But when there is a gap in a father's relationship with God, there will be a gap in his family's relationship with God. When there is no vision, the people will perish, so we need men with vision. Let our children see us praying, going to church, and loving our families.

Chapter 27

Pretentious Insanity

1 Samuel 21:9–15

Haddon Robinson, a professor of preaching at a top seminary, told a story about a Chinese boy who wanted to learn about jade. He studied with a talented teacher who put a piece of jade in his hand and told him to hold it tight. The teacher started talking to him about everything— philosophy, the sun, women, men—all kinds of topics, everything but about jade. After an hour, he took the jade stone back and sent the boy home.

This procedure went on for several weeks. The boy was frustrated and wondered when he would be taught about jade, but he was too polite to ask his teacher.

One day, the teacher put a stone in his hand. The boy cried out instinctively, "This isn't jade!" He had become so familiar with the genuine that he could immediately detect the counterfeit.

What about us? Are we familiar enough with the genuine that we can detect an imposter? Are we familiar enough with true worship that we can detect when worship has become just a show or entertainment? We need to be careful, because Satan majors in making the fake look real (2 Corinthians 11:14); he masquerades as an angel of light. Just because it sounds holy and looks holy doesn't mean it is holy. We must become familiar with the genuine so we can detect what isn't real. We have to watch out for wolves dressed up like sheep because they will draw us close only to devour us with bad doctrine.

Our text finds David the king, the psalmist, the warrior, running for his life from Saul, who wanted to kill him. David allowed fear to diminish his faith in God. He ran for ten years from Nob to Gath, to Adullam and Ziph. He met up with a king, Ahimelech, whom he asked for a weapon. Ahimelech said that the only weapon he had was the sword David had used to cut off Goliath's head. It had not been used since then.

When that happened, one of Saul's spies saw it and informed Saul (1 Samuel 22:9). David fled Nob and went to Gath, where he found himself in the enemy camp. King Achish was a Philistine king, where Goliath was from. The people of Gath started asking, "Isn't that David, the one they sing about? Saul has killed his thousands, but David his ten thousands."

David feared for his life. He had to come up with a scheme to save himself. He pretended to be insane and started acting like a madman. The king said that he was sure he had enough crazy men and didn't need another. David was released.

If we read the entire chapter, we will see that every place David ran, he told a lie out of fear. He acted insane, but lying will always lead to something else. In verse 9, David was running, and it is clear from this verse that he had his old sword in his hands. Whereas as a boy, he had a slingshot, as a man, he had a sword, and he was afraid the sword represented the sword of the Spirit in the New Testament. Here's my point—never run with the sword in your hand.

God has not called us to run away but to go forward and to chase our enemies. Leviticus 26:7 says, "You will pursue your enemies and they will fall by the sword before you." Deuteronomy 32:30 says, "How could one chase a thousand or two put ten thousand to flight, unless their Rock had sold them?" All we need is the Word of the Lord. If we ever forget the Word, we should have enough Scripture in our hearts. If David defeated Goliath with the sword, we can defeat Satan with the sword of the Spirit, the Word of God. Isn't that what Jesus did in the wilderness? The sword is the only offensive weapon in our arsenal;

everything else in Ephesians 6 deals with defense. The sword is our offense as we go forward to meet our enemies.

David pretended to be so insane because of his fear; verse 13 says that he started making marks on the door. I became intrigued with the fact that he was writing on the door. I wondered how he could write if he was insane. I started to do some digging into the text and discovered that David was writing the twenty-second letter of the Hebrew alphabet. We find it right above verse 169 of Psalm 119; the little mark there is what he wrote, and in ancient Hebrew and Phoenician, it was the shape of a cross. While he was pretending to be insane, he was sane enough to know that the cross would keep him safe among his enemies.

That's why even in a bad economy, we have not lost our minds. We still go to church even though we're broke and jobless because the cross keeps us sane. If we just cling to the old, rugged cross, we will make it. He shed his blood for our covering, and we should cling to his blood. The Israelites put lambs' blood on their doors so the death angel would pass over them; they were covered by the blood.

David was called insane by the king in verse 14. Let me say this— never allow the enemy to think he can drive you crazy. If you do, you will go through life as a fake. If you don't fake it, you can do all things through Christ, who strengthens you. You can succeed in life without cheating, lying, or politicking.

And if you find yourself in a bind, don't act crazy to get out of it. Psalm 34:19 says that though many are the afflictions of the righteous, the Lord will deliver them from them all.

Chapter 28

Dropped by a Nurse but Picked Up by a King

2 Samuel 9:1–13

One of my favorite parts of the Christmas story is about the place of the birth of Christ, for even though he was a King, he was not born in a palace, for that would have meant that only kings, princes, queens, and princesses would have had access to him. There was nothing royal about his birth; he was born in a stable surrounded by animals so everyone could have access to him. Even though he started out low, God raised him to the top. There cannot be prejudice in the kingdom.

When Cain killed Abel, God asked him where Abel was. Cain said that he wasn't his brother's keeper. I want to remind us today—yes we are!

All of what we have said thus far takes us into this message about protecting our children Mephibosheth was the crippled son of a prince, Jonathan, and the grandson of a king, Saul. He became crippled when as a child his nurse dropped him. He went through life with a noticeable, severe handicap that precluded him from moving up in the kingdom even though he was the heir apparent.

We find him all grown up after being abused and misused all his life. Destiny brought him into the presence of King David. He and Mephibosheth's grandfather, Saul, were enemies and rivals, but Jonathan, Saul's son, and David were good friends, and one day after David had conquered the Philistines, the Moabites, and the Arameans, he sent for one of Saul's servants to find out if there were any survivors of Saul's house that he could show kindness to. Ziba, the messenger, said, "Well, king, the son of Jonathan is still living, though he has a physical handicap." David remembered that one day a long time ago, he and Jonathan made a covenant we can find in 1 Samuel 20:14–15, when Jonathan asked David to never cut off kindness from his family. Because of that promise, David as the king showed mercy to Mephibosheth, Jonathan's son. This was an unprecedented move on the part of King David; no king had ever shown any compassion for the disadvantaged, but David adopted Mephibosheth as his own.

That's what we need to do with our children today. We need more Christian men and adults who will spiritually adopt each other's children, for they are being taken advantage of. Our children are being kidnapped by the hundreds every year; every year, there are more and more children missing, more and more children being sexually, psychologically, and mentally abused. It's not just happening at the hands of strangers; many of our children are being abused at home by an uncle or a cousin, and that's why the Lord placed upon my heart that as a church we must take a stand against sexual predators and protest the release of sexual offenders back into the same neighborhood where they abused someone. We must protest the release of sexual offenders near schools or playgrounds. If we don't, we pass up opportunities to helping the Mephibosheths who cross our paths every day.

I see hope in this text; if there was hope for a crippled boy in this text, there is hope for every child today. Thank God for King David, who was not going to allow the system to snatch another child. Thank god for King David, who was not going to let another child live a life in despair. Let's see how David helped this boy. Let's see what we can learn.

Mephibosheth had been so abused as a child that even as an adult (verses 4–5), he was still living in obscurity. When David found him, he was living in a place called Lo Debar, which is in Gilead. He was being taken care of by a man by the name of Makir. David brought him out from living in obscurity.

Men, if we are to protect our children, we need to bring them out from living in obscurity. When children encounter misfortune such as abuse, they are told by their abusers not to tell anyone, that it's a secret. They grow up living in obscurity; they walk around at school and at home with hidden secrets because somebody had made them afraid. They live like Mephibosheth in fear, shut off from the world. We need Christian parents who will question their children every day after school about what went on. Did anybody touch you in your private area? Did anybody say anything to you sexually? We need to teach our children that it's all right to talk to us about these things. If not, we're raising children who are living in obscurity.

David pulled Mephibosheth out of obscurity and (in verse 7) gave him everything that belonged to his grandfather. David understood that although Mephibosheth was the heir of his grandfather's throne, he would be unable to get it because he was lame. David blessed the boy with interest (verse 7). First, he gave him everything that belonged to his grandfather. He gave him a seat at his table. That was repayment with interest. That's what our King wants to do with our children; whatever our children have lost, the Lord wants to restore it. But this is not just for children; it's also for adults. Does anybody here need a blessing with interest? Does anyone know what it means that that the Lord has some blessings for us on backlog? He was just holding them for us until we were ready for them, and when he thinks we're ready for them, he will give them to us. He doesn't give them to us all at one time because we couldn't handle them. So he gives us a little here and a little there!

When David does all this for Mephibosheth, it's obvious that Mephibosheth was not used to it; he had endured such verbal abuse because of his handicap that in verse 8, he called himself a dog. Brothers, before we can help our children, we need to reverse the curse by improving their self-esteem. The enemy has used the self-esteem of our children as a curse, so we must reverse the curse by improving the self-esteem of our children, so they don't walk around with their heads down. They should look us in the face when we talk to them. Perhaps they have been told by their abusers that they are nothing and that nobody wants them but the abusers. We need to reverse the curse and tell our children they have been bought with a price, that they are children of God, that they are not sheep without a shepherd, that they were made in his image, and that God don't make no junk.

In verse 13, David brought this crippled man to his table, where Mephibosheth stayed for the rest of his life. This is more than a text about God's ability to provide for us; this verse means that the King will always elevate the abused and misused—it doesn't matter what we have done, it doesn't matter what has happened to us, it doesn't matter what our imperfections are, the King will always elevate the abused and misused. And when he elevates us, we should never settle for leftovers when God has given us a King's menu. We should never settle for less than his caviar, steak, and lamb.

Chapter 29

Grace—The Remedy for Physical Illness

2 Corinthians 12:7–9

Donald Grey Barnhouse, a great preacher, said that love that reaches up is adoration, love that reaches across is affection, and love that reaches down is grace. We all have the opportunity to receive grace; though we cannot reach up and pull God down, God will reach down and pull us up, an act that describes God's grace. His grace rescues us from our bad situations, gives us endurance in sickness, and grants us relief. Some who have survived breast cancer, for instance, attribute it to their doctor, and others attribute it to early detection, but I believe they survived because of God's grace, unmerited favor we cannot earn or ever deserve. God gives it to us freely.

If we have been diagnosed with something we don't know how to handle, we should connect with somebody in church who has already experienced it, whether it's a heart condition or cancer. They are the ones that Bible speaks about in Romans 15:1; the strong must bear the infirmities of the weak. Those who have endured are the strong ones, those who are going through are the weak ones, and when weakness hooks up with strength, the strong will pull us through.

Paul in this text had started to boast and to become conceited because he had just returned from a trip to heaven. In verses 1 through 6, he described his journey and said in essence that he could not tell what he saw, that we'd have to see for ourselves. To keep from boasting, he described what is called a thorn in the flesh he said was sent to him from Satan. But actually, as was the case with Job, Satan was the immediate cause but God was the ultimate cause. God sent him a constant reminder through the thorn in the flesh. We are not sure what this thorn was. Some theologians have suggested a chronic sickness like migraine headaches or eye problems, for Paul had been converted on the Damascus road and was blinded for three days. He could have been still dealing with the effects of that. In Galatians 6:11, he wrote about writing in large letters because he had a problem with his eyes.

One thing is clear: God allowed Paul's thorn to teach him humility. When was the last time we had a good lesson on humility? Perhaps Paul is not the only one who needed a thorn in the flesh; some of us do too. It's easy to forget how we made it over, it's easy to act pious now that we've arrived. It's easy to hang out with the rich and famous and look down on the poor and unknown. John Bradford, a sixteenth-century preacher, once saw criminals going to the scaffold and said in effect, "There but for the grace of God go I." Paul said in 1 Corinthian 15:10, "I persecuted the church but by Grace of God I am what I am." In other words, he could have been dead, in jail, strung out except for the grace of God.

When Paul was going through his debilitating circumstance, he said in verse 8, "I asked the Lord three times. I pleaded with the Lord to take away from me" (stop there). God did not honor his request. Unanswered prayers don't always mean that the need is not met; in fact, we sometimes get greater blessings when God does not answer our prayers. Sometimes, he leaves us in situations long enough to teach us a lesson, and at other times he leaves us in things because the longer we are in them, the longer we focus on him, and he gets the glory. He might not always answer the prayer, but he will always answer the need. What do you need today? Healing? He will answer that. Food? He will answer that. Financial security? He will answer that.

Watch how God answered Paul's prayer: "My grace is sufficient for you." There is no substitute for grace; it's not luck, it's not coincidence, it's not déjà vu—it's just grace. God has a way of proving this because every now and then, when he moves to prevent us from giving something or someone else the credit, he will leave indelible impressions on us. That's why I believe Paul in Galatians 2:20 wrote that he had been crucified with Christ, but then in Galatians 6:17, he wrote that he bore on his body the marks of the Lord Jesus—grace marks.

Thank God for those grace marks. If we have had surgery, our scars may never go away, but every time we need to be reminded of just how good God is, we should look at the scar and say, "Thank you for my grace mark, God. I'm a survivor, I'm an over comer, I'm a new creature."

Chapter 30

Roadside Assistance

Mark 10:46–52

Sally Colin, a mother of three who lived in Fort Smith, Arkansas, was blind due to a disease. Her oldest child, a fifteen-year-old named Christopher, took care of his mother and his younger siblings. She would depend on him to get around, and he worked at a convenience store stacking soda and ice for $20 a week so he could help supplement his mother's public assistance check. One day, she started feeling sorry for herself and complained to her son. He said, "Mom, I will always be your eyes."

One day, Christopher was hit by a car and died. His family agreed to donate his organs, and Dr. Robert Knox transplanted Christopher's corneas into his mother's eyes. A week after Christopher's death, a week after the transplant, Sally Colin opened her eyes and saw her children for the first time in thirteen years. She saw Christopher's report card and saw he was on the honor roll. She began to cry. She realized her son had kept his promise to always be her eyes.

Over two thousand years ago, Jesus Christ said he would never leave us or forsake us. His eyes became ours, his hands became ours, his feet became ours. This is why Acts 17:28 says for in him we live, move, and have our being.

Jesus healed a blind man on the road. Have you ever been stranded on the road? Ever run out of gas or had a flat in the middle of nowhere?

These are cumbersome, inconvenient events, but thank God; his roadside assistance, his AAA, is always on call 24-7. Our inconveniences are opportunities for God to come to our rescue. We are surrounded with people with good eyesight but are spiritually blind. Today, the Lord is willing to come to your rescue.

The setting of our text is Jericho, a few miles from Jerusalem. It was one of the most influential cities of Palestine. The incident with the blind man took place during Passover or Lent. This was one of Jesus' last healings prior to Holy Week.

Since it was Passover, the blind man knew that a crowd of pilgrims and religious people would be going through Jericho on their way to Jerusalem. Jesus came through with a crowd. The blind had heard crowds before, but this one sounded different. He inquired and discovered that Jesus was passing through; he wanted to get in his way because he had heard about him. He cried, "Lord, have mercy on me." His name was Bartimaeus, son of Timaeus which means "son of a blind man"; he was the blind son of a blind father, which could mean that when the son was healed, so would the father be. John 8:36 says who the Son sets free is free indeed, and not just that person but his or her whole household, family, and generation as well. Jesus came to bind up the enemy and to break generational curses. It's an all-in-the-family healing.

Bartimaeus called for Christ from the roadside in verse 46. He had an emergency, and in Jesus' mind, the cries of his children are always emergencies. Even if it seems small to us, it is paramount to the Lord; no circumstance is too small for him; they are all 911 moments for Jesus. When we call him, he will stop what he is doing and come see about us.

Our nation is in a state of emergency. Marijuana is legal in some places, eight states have made same-sex marriages legal, anybody can get a gun, and sex education is being taught in some elementary schools. Teenagers can get abortions some places without their parents knowing about it. Somebody call 911!

When Bartimaeus heard it was Jesus, he began to cry, "Have mercy on me." Here, misery didn't love company, it loved mercy. He asked Jesus not for food, water, housing, or clothes but for mercy. He relied on Christ's compassion because he understood what he needs was much more than sight; he realized he needed spiritual healing much more than physical healing, for the spiritual healing must precede physical healing.

Jesus could have restored his sight but if he didn't have spiritual healing first, he would be able to see but still be blind. If we don't have faith in Jesus Christ, we are blind anyway. Bartimaeus was shouting, "Have mercy on me!" The more they told him to be quiet, the louder he shouted. Don't let anybody suppress your shout, for they don't know your testimony, and they don't know what you have been through, for if they did, they would be shouting too.

In verse 50, when Jesus heard all the commotion, he probably made the same ones who were telling Bartimaeus to be quiet to call him. They said to Bartimaeus, "Cheer up! He's calling you." Here's the part I like. Throwing his cloak aside, he jumped to his feet and went to Jesus. When Jesus calls, we should get there any way we can.

Bartimaeus knew this was not a social call but a call for a cure, this was not a call for small talk but for healing. He took off his cloak so it wouldn't trip him up. Sometimes, we too have to free ourselves of our conceit so it won't trip us up.

Jesus healed him, but it wasn't because of his shout, it wasn't because of his begging, and it wasn't because Jesus felt sorry for him. Jesus healed him because of his faith. And it was a healing without touch. To prove that he was healed, the man followed Jesus on the road without assistance.

Sometimes, we have to start following him right from the place where we were healed. Maybe that was in a hospital room, or a car, or a pew in church. One way or another, we have to turn those places into our healing sanctuaries and start following Jesus right from there. We should not wait until the next Sunday, for Sunday should be the end result of what we should have been doing all week.

Chapter 31

Walking Miracles

Acts 14:8–11

C. S. Lewis, the great twentieth-century apologist for the church, defined a miracle as an interference with the natural by the supernatural. Let's put it in perspective for us today. Perhaps we didn't have the money or the GPA to get into that ivy league school. We really shouldn't have been accepted, but there was an interference with the natural by the supernatural, and we did. We were in a car wreck that totaled our car but left us unhurt. There was no way we should have survived, but there was an interference with the natural by the supernatural. Some of us would still be alcoholics or drug addicts, but there was an interference with the natural by the supernatural. Today, we are all walking miracles because we all walked through bad things but are still here.

We are men with golf ball mentalities. The first golf balls had smooth surfaces, but then they discovered that golf balls that had been roughed up would travel farther, so they started manufacturing them with dimpled covers.

So it is with life. It takes some rough spots to help us go farther. When we're persecuted, attacked, lied on, and even just misunderstood, it simply means that the Lord is getting ready as men to take us farther on the job, in our faith, in the church, and in our marriages. Every blow we receive will end up giving us more distance. Matthew said that we were blessed when men reviled and persecuted us and said all manner of evil against us. We should rejoice and be glad for great will be our reward in heaven. I know many men who will be rewarded for having been knocked around. When I think things over, I can truly say I have been blessed, I have a testimony. We are blessed today not only because we have clothes and homes but also because we just have air to breathe. That's a blessing!

The setting of our text is in a place called Lystra, in what is now Turkey. Paul and Barnabas were on their first missionary journey and end up there because they were driven out of Iconium for trying to evangelize. The people of Lystra were superstitious pagans who believed in and worshipped Greek gods; they had built a temple to Zeus, the father of the Greek gods.

The people there were so accustomed to the religiously spectacular that they attempted to give the Greek gods credit for something God had done. In verse 11, after the crippled man was healed, they said that their gods had come down to us in human form, but God himself tells us in Isaiah 42:8, "I am the Lord that is my name and my glory and I will not share my glory neither will I give my Praise to an idol." Too many of us do the same thing; when God does something for us, we say we have made it this far because of who we know, politics, and education. No. It was God and God alone. Watch what God did.

The man, who had been crippled from birth, listened to Paul preach. When Paul realized the man had faith, he told him to stand. The man jumped up first, he skipped before he began to walk. When God speeds up the process, we can jump before we walk, just as this man did. He skipped, but what I mean is that he skipped—he passed up— rehabilitation, physical therapy, crawling, crutches, braces, a cane, and just jumped before he walked.

God, in his mercy and compassion, will allow us to skip some things and still make it to the top. The thief on the cross skipped communion, catechism, and baptism and went right to heaven with Jesus.

In Genesis 5, Enoch walked with God and he was all of a sudden not there because God had taken him; God actually allowed him to skip death. Just skip before you leap; in fact, don't even wait in line. Just skip to the front of the line, for the Bible says in Matthew 20:16 the last shall be first and the first shall be last. If you keep being faithful, God will allow you to skip some things.

As Paul preached, the crippled man was listening. When Paul told him to stand, he must have spoken in Hebrew, for Paul was a Jew, and the man spoke a dialect of Greek. they couldn't understand each other. Romans 10:17 is clear that faith comes by hearing and hearing by the Word of God. What Paul did here was something that had never been done in this man's life; Paul affirmed in Proverbs 18:21 that death and life are in the power of the tongue. We are not called to crucify with our tongues. How many people have we killed this week with our tongues? How many young people who were already down and dealing with self-esteem issues did we make feel even worse? How many have come to church and left crippled by our words?

We are called to speak life. This man was not only unable to walk, he was not saved, but in one word, Paul gave him double for his trouble. Just a word from the Lord will make everything all right even if we don't understand it, for the Holy Spirit is our interpreter.

When the man jumped up, he was affirming Isaiah 35:6, which tells us that the lame shall leap like deer. This man was leaping as a tangible sign that we should never get complacent with where we are, that we should leap into new environments. Some need to leap out of abusive relationships and into restoring relationships. Some need to leap out of financial strongholds and into financial freedom. Some should leap into their futures because they are in storms in the present.

We can leap from bondage into freedom, from sadness to happiness, from darkness into marvelous light. We should not stop leaping until we see Jesus with his arms wide open saying, "Come unto me, all you who labor and are heavy laden and I will give you rest."

A daughter was driving her father, a pastor, to preach. They were driving through a bad storm, and the daughter said, "Daddy, I need to pull over because the storm is too bad." The father said no. He wanted her to keep driving. But the weather got worse. "Daddy, I can't see in this storm. I think I need to stop." The father told her to keep driving.

She drove a few more miles, and it started to hail. They looked in the rearview mirror and saw that all the traffic had pulled over. The daughter prepared to do the same, but her father told her to keep driving because they were near their destination.

When they arrived to the church, the father told his daughter to look back at all of those cars and eighteen-wheelers still stopped. "They stopped," he said, "but because you kept driving, you're no longer in the storm."

Keep on driving through sickness and through pain, because the storm is passing over.

Chapter 32

Providential Prayers for Presidential Leadership (Inauguration Sermon in Honor of President Barack Obama)

1 Timothy 2:1–2

The world has witnessed history, and many of us were there when President Barack Obama took the oath and was sworn in as the forty-fourth president of the United States of America. It was probably one of the most historic events of our time, one that our children and their children will remember for the rest of their lives.

And I just want us for a moment to deliberate and ruminate over the history that has just been made. Do you realize that President Obama was sworn in on the same steps where forty-five years prior, Dr. Martin Luther King Jr. articulated his "I Have a Dream" speech? He was sworn in on the same steps that were built by slaves; that's right—slaves built the White House, about four hundred self-educated carpenters named Ben, Harry, Peter, and Daniel (no last names because they were property). A black, self-educated mathematician by the name of Benjamin Banneker was the chief project manager. He was in charge of the building process; he was the only one who could read blueprints, and he was good with numbers.

I don't think we comprehend how historical this present moment in time is, for slaves were a common sight in the White House from the time it was built in 1795. At least twelve presidents owned slaves, including George Washington, Ulysses Grant, Thomas Jefferson, Andrew Jackson, James Madison, and James Monroe.

There is another piece of history I want to deposit in our spirits as we celebrate this historic occasion. I didn't have the privilege of going to Washington, DC, for the inauguration, but those who did and stood on the mall, the large tract of land running through downtown Washington that links the capitol and the Lincoln Memorial, were standing on the place where slaves had been bought and sold. We today shop at malls, but before the Civil War, the mall in our capital was where slaves were bought and sold. That's why we get so excited about our new president; his elevation is an elevation for every minority that has been disenfranchised, marginalized, discriminated against, or abused, for God is a God of the oppressed.

In this text, Paul was urging the Ephesian church to pray for all men, especially those who were in authority. This is interesting; Paul wrote this he was referring to Nero, the Roman emperor then who loathed Christians and blamed them for the fire that devastated Rome in AD 64. While the Jews and Romans were at war, Nero persecuted Christians. Paul was imprisoned and appeared before Nero. Upon his release, he realized there was growing acrimony and a deteriorating political atmosphere, but he still urged the Ephesians to pray for kings and all those in authority.

Even though we may be on opposite ends of the spectrum, some of us Republicans and others Democrats, we have been called to pray providential prayers for presidential leadership. Providence is God's care and foresight over the world. Leadership is the act of empowering those around us to achieve their goals. We should be praying for our commander and chief, so let us pray for our president.

In this text, the central theme is prayer. During these next four years, praying for our church and our nation should be of utmost importance. The church should make prayer a priority. It is sad to see that prayer has lost its relevance in worship; it has taken a backseat to announcements, offerings, processionals and the recessionals, and the greeting of visitor. This is what Paul was trying to impress upon Timothy in this text. Timothy was promoting programs, pleasing people, and practicing church politics, but he wasn't praying, and Paul was telling him to get back to the Word, to prayer, and train the people to do the same.

When we pray for our president, I want us to remember what his name means. In Swahili and Arabic, *barak* means "blessed," but in Hebrew, his name has a different meanings. In Hebrew there are at least seven different levels of praise, including *halal*, which means "boastful." We get our word *hallelujah* from this. *Zamar* means praise. Then there is *shabach*, which means "to shout." This makes the Devil shut up (Psalm 47:1).

The one I like is the Hebrew word *barak*, "to kneel, bow, and bless God,"—it's time to get our knees and pray. When God elevated Barack Obama to the highest office in the land, that was his way of saying to the church to stay on its knees. He elevated a black man so that every time we looked at him, we would not see him but what God had done. I like what Williams Cowper, an English poet said: "Satan trembles when he sees the weakest Christian on their knees."

When this text says we need to pray for kings and all those in authority, I believe it means we need to pray for their success. God told Joshua in Joshua 1:8 that he had to meditate on the Law day and night to achieve success. This should be our prayer for our new president. Let's pray that he meditates on the Word day and night and does not become so presidential that he is not spiritual. Let's pray that he continues to love his wife and his children and that the First Family gets in a church home and influences others to go to church. Let's pray that, just like Barak in Judges 4 who defeated the Canaanites and was successful in war, God brings President Obama success.

This says to me that we should also pray for the safety of our First Family. Yes, I know the Secret Service will be with them twenty-four hours a day, but I want us to pray that God will dispatch his angels to protect the First Family and the Secret Service people themselves.

Let's pray that the angels will watch over the First Family, protect their daughters when they are at school, protect the First Lady as she speaks, and protect the president as he governs!

(This sermon has been placed in the National Library of Congress.)